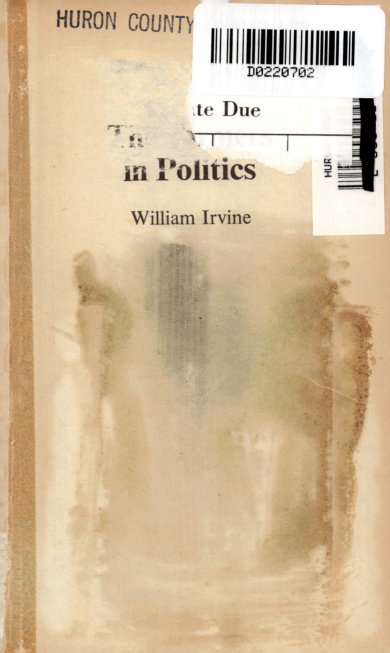

D0220702

in Politics

William Irvine

The Farmers
in Politics

William Irvine

With an Introduction
by Reginald Whitaker

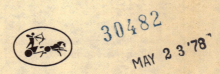

The Carleton Library No. 114
Published by McClelland and Stewart
Limited in association with the
Institute of Canadian Studies,
Carleton University

THE CARLETON LIBRARY

A series of reprints, original works and new
collections of source material relating to Canada,
issued under the editorial supervision of the Institute
of Canadian Studies of Carleton University, Ottawa.

©*McClelland and Stewart Limited, 1976*

ISBN 0-7710-9810-3

The Farmers in Politics was first published
by McClelland and Stewart in 1920.

The Canadian Publishers
McClelland and Stewart Limited
25 Hollinger Road, Toronto

Printed and bound in Canada

INTRODUCTION TO THE CARLETON LIBRARY EDITION

Canada, according to the familiar legend, is a country singularly without political ideology. Political ideologies are believed to be, like venereal diseases, the result of moral decay, and characteristic of the decadent areas of the world, such as Europe. Here, in the clean frontier atmosphere of North America, there seems little evidence of such weaknesses. Instead of ideology, the Canadian password has been *pragmatism*. Our politics have been those of brokerage parties which seek to aggregate the largest number of disparate interests behind the most nebulous platform possible, and political decision makers have been guided not by dogma but by a practical appreciation of what will work in a given situation.[1] So the legend goes.

There is, of course, a large element of truth in this image. Few would deny that Canadian politics have been lacking in ideological clarity. There is also an uncomfortable awareness, even among those who laud the rejection of ideology, that our politics have been without principles and moral commitment.[2] Yet the picture is overdrawn, on both sides. The simple two-party model of contending factions distinguished only by their status as either "Ins" or "Outs" still has the ring of reality about it. At the same time, third parties basing their existence on an ideological rejection of the major parties have been a permanent feature of the national and many provincial scenes since the end of the First World War, and have attracted the considerable attention of social scientists for many years. Moreover, the use of the label "pragmatism," like a coat of paint, may conceal a host of sins, in this case ideological sins. The politics of pragmatism in many cases prove to have been the politics of mystification, serving particular interests while piously denying that politics is about the advancement of certain interests against others.

A number of revisionist works have described the domination of Canadian public life by the interests of corporate capitalism, utilizing a panoply of ideological weapons, including "apolitical" or "pragmatic" politics, to consolidate this domination.[3] This in turn suggests a further dimension to the question of ideology. Ideological politics inevitably implies *class* politics:

contending ideologies arise from differentiated social and economic classes within a given society, representing differing images of how the resources of that society should be divided, and of the kind of human relationships considered desirable. Hand in hand with the denial of ideology has gone a denial of the class basis of Canadian society. The myth of classlessness, which has been recently subjected to such devastating attack as to be no longer defensible,[4] served the dual historical role of obscuring both the actual perceptions of the weaker classes of their own situation, and of mystifying in retrospect the real impact on Canadian politics of class issues and class ideologies.

The great upheaval in Canadian politics at the end of the First World War is at the same time the most startling example of the power of class politics in this country, and the most extraordinary example of the ability of the pragmatist school to argue away the material evidence of class and ideology as important factors in our politics. The end of the old two-party system, the rapid and highly successful organization at both the federal and provincial levels of a new party around a distinct class base and in support of a set of ideas whose radical divergence from the conventional wisdom of the old parties certainly justifies the term "ideology"—these are facts of some significance in assessing the nature of political development in this country. The sudden explosion of the farmers into politics, with consequences the reverberations of which are still heard today, was a crucial event in the shaping of the Canadian political culture.

William Irvine's *The Farmers in Politics* was published in 1920, at the high tide of political success for the farmers' movement. It remains a lucid statement of the distinctive ideological position of the farmers, seen from the partisan but lively left wing of the movement. A neglected classic of political polemic, the book calls for reassessment in the light of our current understanding of the political circumstances at the time of its publication. It is also of interest for what it reveals of its author. Irvine personally embodied a wide range of enthusiasms, ideas, and tendencies which animated the small but voluble left wing of Canadian politics in the first half of the twentieth century. He was a preacher, journalist, pamphleteer, Member of Parliament, political organizer, agitator, and playwright.

This introductory essay will attempt first to situate the farmers' movement at the end of the war within the context of the developing Canadian political economy, then to briefly examine some of the major themes of the book itself, and finally to outline Irvine's subsequent career in the light of the failure of the farmers' movement of the post-war period and the resultant search for better forms of political expression.

The Roots of Farmer Radicalism

The first, and undoubtedly the most important, analytical approach to Canadian political economy is the staples model of economic development associated with W. A. Mackintosh, Harold Innis and others, and the Laurentian school of historical development which is connected to it. The staples model, emphasizing single resource extraction (fur, timber, cod, wheat) within an imperialist framework, has become part of the wider literature on economic development, constituting perhaps one of the most important contributions of Canada to international scholarship. The decline of this approach in the 1950's and 1960's coincided with a general decline in the entire concept of political economy, as distinct from either economics or political science.[5] In the present decade, there has been a revival of this older tradition of scholarship which looks to the interrelationship of economic and political factors as the basis of historical development. One of the most important strands in this revival has been a tendency on the part of younger scholars to fuse the staples model with the class concepts of Marxism.[6]

However much the staples approach has taught us about the basis of economic development, it has also generated a certain metropolitan and upper class bias to the understanding of the political responses to economic changes, as so conservative a scholar as W. L. Morton long ago pointed out.[7] Locating the dynamic of development squarely in the metropolitan merchant class of the St. Lawrence, or in its successors in the Toronto-Montreal financial and industrial bourgeoisie, is a crucial step in identifying the source of capitalist development, but the focus tends to miss the reactions of those on the receiving end— reactions which have been very important factors indeed in the shaping of the Canadian political economy. Marxist analysis, as a method, recognizes a dynamic, or internal logic, in the development of capitalism as a system; and it sees this dynamic in terms of class differentiation and conflict. To employ a much misused term, this type of analysis is *dialectical*; that is, it attempts to comprehend both actions and reactions and to lo-cate the specificity of a particular political economy in the interplay of these factors.

To say that North American society has developed differently from Europe is to state the obvious. Yet simply because the classic Marxist class conflict between the organized working class and the capitalist owners of the means of production has been much more pronounced in Europe than on this continent is no reason to assume that class conflict has been absent from North American politics. The question must rather be posed in terms of which classes have been important in North American economic development, and whether their interests have been significant factors in structuring the politics of the time.[8] In Canada, the relative weakness of the working class as an auton-omous agent of political change is not seriously to be disputed — at least in relation to Europe, although perhaps not in relation to the United States. But this does not mean that class has been without significance, certainly not with regard to the dominant classes, as the literature of the merchants and financiers of the central Canadian metropole clearly indicates, but no less with regard to the dominated classes.

It was a universal comment in the nineteenth century that in Europe land was dear and labour was cheap, but that in North America, land was cheap and labour dear.[9] This establishes a crucial point of divergence between the two continents in class terms. It was difficult to keep people in the labour force and off the land in the new world. Despite ill-conceived Tory schemes for creating landed aristocracies and established churches backed by clergy reserves in the early colonial history of Can-ada, the country developed a largely agricultural economy with the family farm as the typical unit of production. Not until the 1921 census did the urban share of the Canadian population finally rival the rural proportion. The 1901 census showed that 89 percent of all farms in Canada were operated by their own-ers.[10] In Marxist terms, this meant that there was by European standards a very large and economically significant group of independent commodity producers — a "petite bourgeoisie," standing apart from either capital or labour.

As early as the 1820's and 1830's some of the elements of class conflict between the independent farmers and the growing commercial and financial interests of the dominant groups (symbolized by the Family Compact and the Chateau Clique) were apparent. Although numerous other factors, such as religion and ethnicity, were germane to the political conflicts which flared into open rebellion in 1837-38, very specific class issues as perceived by small farmers were featured in the manifestos and political programmes of the rebels. The complaints of the farmers tended to concentrate on political and economic griev-ances, among which the problem of credit was particularly prominent. It is of course impossible to generalize about the economic situation of the small family farmer over the whole of the nineteenth century, but some factors stand out. The ques-tion of the capital necessary for investment in land and equip-ment was crucial. It was at this point that the "independent" producer became vulnerable to financial capital through the credit market. The price of the produce was of course subject to the vicissitudes of the market, and storage, transportation, and marketing were additional areas where the farmers' control over their return became subject to powerful outside forces.

To the extent that the dominant forces of capitalism were successful in the late nineteenth century in their attempts to industrialize the country, the agricultural sector was doomed to relative decline and depopulation. Along with the consolidation of farms, and heavier capitalization, agricultural production was drawn ever more tightly into the web of the wider capitalist market. In the long run this is exactly what did happen, but there was an important counter-trend. The National Policy of the Macdonald Conservatives, later extended and broadened by the Laurier Liberals, had as one of its central tenets the incor-poration of the western prairies into the national economy as a producer of agricultural exports to gain foreign exchange in world markets, as well as to provide a domestic market for the protected manufacturing industries of central Canada. Out of this policy was formed a vast agricultural hinterland, with wheat as its staple cash crop, in an inferior and subservient position to the central Canadian metropole. The seeds of agrarian radical-ism in the west thus grew in a soil of class resentment enriched by regional identity.

If capitalism destroyed the feudal order in Europe, and with it the landed aristocracy and the peasants who worked the fields, it created a new dialectic of class antagonism with its development of a landless labour force filling the mines and factories of the Industrial Revolution. In Canada, there was no feudal past and no peasantry. Nevertheless, capitalism created its own antagonists, through the logic of its own growth. The beginnings of an industrial working class and the development of a large independent commodity producer class, both in an economic and political position of domination by corporate capitalism, set the state for the emergence of professions, particularly teaching, preaching and journalism, which were in a somewhat problematic relationship to the dominant forces of capitalism, and were feared by these forces as unruly and untrustworthy agitational elements.[11] The rise of the "Social Gospel," the radical left wing of Christianity spread by men consciously imbued with feelings of solidarity towards the lower orders, and the increasing salience of such issues as feminism in mobilizing the interest and support of sizeable sectors of the population, indicated that by the time of the First World War Canadians were in a process of reappraisal of their underlying social and political values.

The war itself greatly accelerated the changes already initiated by the rapid industrialization of the previous two decades. By war's end, there was such pent-up frustration and desire for change that a sense of impending upheaval was pervasive throughout the society. The outpouring of books and pamphlets on the "social question" at this time was unprecedented in a nation little disposed toward introspection and social criticism.[12] This intellectual concern was matched by political activism and grass-roots militancy on a scale never before witnessed. From the explosion of the farmers into political prominence to the Winnipeg General Strike, the lower orders, hitherto reasonably passive, were on the move—although in what direction no one could positively say. Abroad the picture was even more disconcerting to those familiar with the certitudes of the nineteenth century: the convulsion of world war had brought in its wake the Russian Revolution, and the year 1919 saw a series of revolutionary uprisings across Europe. The old world was coming adrift from its moorings.

In the end, the storm passed, and the old order reasserted itself, albeit in a modified and modernized form. Out of the political upheaval in Canada came not revolution, but William Lyon Mackenzie King and the Liberal party. Capitalism had faced the challenge, and the mid-1920s, the forces of radicalism seemed spent on all fronts. Yet a decade later, by the 1935 election, with capitalism reeling from the effects of the Great Depression, it had become clear that the simple two-party brokerage system had been lost forever, and that a social democratic third party, the CCF, had arrived on the scene, thus distinguishing Canada from the United States, where the Socialist party had disappeared from national politics, never to return. Both the weakness and the tenacity of the radicalism generated in the early twentieth century must be taken into account in the historical balance sheet. Radical political action fell far, far short of transforming the structure of the Canadian political economy, yet it did leave an imprint on the shape of Canadian politics.

To understand the specific nature of radicalism as it actually developed in Canada, it is first necessary to analyse the concrete class forces which went into the left-wing upsurge. The fact that the most impressive political confrontation of corporate capitalism mounted in this century came not from the organized working class, as occurred in Europe, but from the aroused farmers is of signal importance in the shaping of radical thought. The Winnipeg General Strike of 1919, the sympathetic strikes carried out in other western cities, and the emergence of some elements of labour political representation in both federal and provincial politics did indicate the appearance of a class consciousness among industrial workers. But this was very incomplete and tentative; moreover, the industrial working class was simply not large enough at the end of the war to be of such strategic importance to the Canadian economy as was the working class of more advanced industrial nations. The farmers were a different story. Larger in numbers, strategically placed both in economic and political terms, and demonstrating a high degree of solidarity and collective purpose, the farmers were poised at an historical moment of great potential for political change.

The world view of the farmers, the ideological image of the well-ordered society derived from their particular class position and life experience, was one which allowed a significant divergence from the orthodoxy propagated by the dominant forces of capitalism and accepted by the mainstream of society. The farmers' movement did involve the vision of a better world that was indeed radical by the standards of the time. It would be false to suggest that all the farmers held such a view; even the leaders of the movement were deeply divided on its goals. Like any large social movement of radical tendency, there were many motives and many expectations assembled under the same umbrella. The point is that advanced ideas were generated by advanced thinkers; such ideas were not simply disembodied rhetoric but found resonance in the larger movement. The *movement* was precisely that: a group of people in motion, in search of a better life, open and questioning. It is in this situation that the true seedbed of radical social and political thought is to be found. Just as in Europe, where periods of revolutionary change such as the English Civil War and the French Revolution have been the periods generating the greatest contributions to political philosophy, so too the period of political unrest and agitation at the end of the First World War in Canada, while far from a revolutionary era, nevertheless generated some original ideas about reforming and transforming the Canadian political economy.

The crucial importance of the farmers at this point of political and ideological flux can scarcely be overestimated for the shaping of left-wing political ideas. The most politically advanced elements of the working class movement were forced to choose sides in a struggle predominantly featuring the large bourgeoisie of central Canada, along with its middle-class allies, against the petite bourgeoisie led by the independent commodity producers of the western wheat provinces and rural Ontario. Not surprisingly, they chose the side of those farmers struggling for what was called "economic democracy," under the leadership and ideological hegemony of a class whose interests and outlook were significantly different from those of the organized working class. There has been a certain tendency on the part of present day Marxists to decry this historical conjuncture as having drawn the working class movement away from its proper socialist path and towards an inappropriate petit bourgeois mentality. Yet to dismiss the farmers and their world as of no interest is an injustice. They were people with a way of life, traditions, culture, and their own hopes and dreams. They went down before the implacable onslaught of the market, of industrialization and urbanization, but they went down fighting, with some dignity and not a little imagination in their stand against the forces oppressing them.[13] Certainly they and their leaders mounted a more impressive counterattack than the organized working class or its leaders have ever mounted against some of these same forces.

As Mackenzie King knew well, the forces of technological liberalism and the capitalist market had indeed doomed the farmers to eventual extinction as a significant political force. His book, *Industry and Humanity*, leaped forward across the decades to a time when the independent commodity producer class had virtually disappeared, and the major confrontation in society was squarely between capital and labour, to a society in fact in which this axis of conflict had become so decisive that the entire political structures of decision-making were to be transformed to embody these collective interests.[14] Yet King himself spent his first years in office as Prime Minister driven by the necessity of finding compromises and common fronts with the representatives of the farmers while the labour question was far down the agenda. And when a social democratic party finally came to birth in the early years of the depression, it was as a farmer-labour alliance, and its founding convention was held in Regina, in the midst of an almost entirely unindustrialized, wheat growing province. Many have argued that this alliance imparted a particular tone to the new party, which has helped shape its philosophy since. On the other hand, the same class of independent commodity producers also turned rightward in politics in other places and other times. The sudden reversion of Ontario farmers back to traditional two-party politics by the mid-1920s, Social Credit in Alberta, the conservatism of the United Farmers government in Manitoba, the Tory populism of John Diefenbaker on the prairies in the 1950s and 1960s, all demonstrate the ambiguity of the farmers' perception of politics, the curious oscillation of views from left to right, the Janus-faced conservative-radicalism of the farmers in politics.

It is precisely at this point, where the farmers' movement overlapped with radical, labour politics that the ideas of William Irvine become highly relevant. An examination of Irvine's career and the evolution of his thought helps cast considerable light upon this complex historical question.

William Irvine, 1885-1962
William Irvine was born in the Shetland Islands and left school early to serve an apprenticeship as a carpenter and boatbuilder. A brief sojourn in the United States, where he worked on the construction site of the St. Louis World's Fair, ended in his return home, where he turned to the Methodist ministry while assimilating a good deal of labour and socialist literature. Recruited by the father of J. S. Woodsworth, later the first leader of the CCF, Irvine came to Canada in 1907 and graduated from Manitoba and Wesley Colleges in 1914 in theology. The author of a recent personal sketch of Irvine suggests that even at this stage in his career, he was "more interested in the social gospel of such teachers and friends as J. S. Woodsworth and Salem Bland than he was in theological dogma."[15] His socialist activities led to a heresy trial and his resignation of his ministry in a small Ontario town in 1916.

Irvine moved to Calgary to take up an offer from the Unitarian Church, which specified that he was to spend 10 per cent of his time on the religious needs of his congregation and the remaining 90 per cent on community work.[16] This was exactly the proper mix to suit Irvine, who threw himself into the seething cauldron of radicalism that was the West in those days with an enthusiasm, dedication, wit and intelligence matched by few others. One of his first activities was journalism, as he helped found a sparkling radical newspaper called *The Nutcracker*, later the *Alberta Non-Partisan*, later still the *Western Independent*. It was an exciting time of new ideas and burning social criticism; during the same period, Calgary also supported another "underground" newspaper of lively and mordant wit—the celebrated, though much less political, *Eyeopener*, edited by the flamboyant and somewhat dissolute Bob Edwards.

The farmers of Alberta had been smarting from the defeat of reciprocity and the victory of protectionist Toryism in the 1911 election, along with a host of other grievances centering around the marketing, storage, and transportation of grain, and the ubiquitous credit system with its high interest rates and foreclosures on mortgages. Irvine's first direct political intervention was as secretary of the Alberta Nonpartisan League, an offshoot of the left wing farmers' movement in North Dakota, which had swept into office in that state in 1916. The League acted as an initial impetus in Alberta for direct political action by farmers, two members being elected in the 1917 provincial election. As its name implied, the League focussed its attacks on the party system, and looked to a non-partisan "business" government in which delegates voted according to the wishes of their constituents and not at the behests of party whips.[17] This importation of political principles which were apparently more appropriate to the American division of powers, where the executive did not depend upon the partisan support of the legislature, than to the British system of cabinet government, was to have a long and paralyzing influence on the farmers' movement in both provincial and federal Canadian politics.

The Nonpartisan League did succeed in drawing the United Farmers of Alberta (UFA), originally a non-political farm organization, into direct political action, despite the reluctance of Alberta farm leader Henry Wise Wood, with whom Irvine had some serious disagreements. The UFA took over from the League as the political arm of the farmers, while Irvine continued to agitate for farmer-labour unity, eventually gaining election to the House of Commons as a "Labour" candidate with UFA backing. Despite his crucial role in encouraging UFA political action, Irvine left Alberta for seven months near the end of 1920, to organize for the farmers' movement in New Brunswick. It was in his absence that *The Farmers in Politics* appeared and was reviewed in the western press, thus keeping his name and ideas before the people of Alberta. Upon his return to Calgary, he threw himself into feverish political activity as the UFA swept to provincial power in the 1921 election, and he himself won a federal seat a few months later.

Coming as it did only a year after the stunning victory of the United Farmers of Ontario in that province's general election, and on the eve of the Alberta victory, followed by a farmer government in Manitoba in 1922, and just before the displacement of the Conservatives as the second largest grouping in the House of Commons by the farmer-based Progressive party in the 1921 national election, *The Farmers in Politics* was obviously a topical book. It endures as one of the most lucid statements of a distinctive class and ideological approach to Canadian politics, which with passion, wit, and relentless vigour seeks to demolish the great Canadian myths of classlessness and pragmatism. It has, moreover, much to say about the historical problem of the relationship of the farmers as a class to the development of radical and socialist politics. The latter point is somewhat paradoxical, since Irvine himself was neither a farmer nor of farming background. As an outsider and an intellectual, Irvine may have overstated the case for the group which he claimed to represent. Certainly, many of the farmers themselves were far more conservative and moderate than Irvine's picture would tend to suggest. Yet at the same time, this defect may have been a virtue, in the sense that Irvine was able to draw out with considerable clarity some of the inarticulate assumptions of the farmers' movement that perhaps only an outsider could discern.

The book did play a modest role in the events which reshaped Western Canadian politics. Yet, even if one is sceptical of the ultimate importance of books in changing the world, it must be said that this is a book which reflected a current of political activism which did in some ways change the Canadian political world. Coming at the full tide of the farmers' politicization, the book is less a theoretical treatise than an expression of the fusion of theory and practice: the articulation of the more advanced ideas associated with a genuine mass protest movement. This places it firmly within the Canadian tradition of political writing, for until very recently Canadians have been very little given to abstract theorizing about the political order and have confined themselves to reflecting upon practical political activities. What *The Farmers in Politics* does demonstrate is that this genre need not be lacking in imaginative innovation. It did involve a serious attempt at a social and political theory which rather outdid the most advanced sections of the farmers' movement.[18]

Richard Allen has written that the "most striking aspect" of Irvine's book "was not so much the exposition of his concept of group government, as the mixture of his political and economic arguments with the religious concepts of the radical social gospel."[19] In fact, compared to such social gospel tracts as Salem Bland's *The New Christianity*, Irvine's book is rather more striking for its dominantly secular tone. Aside from an obligatory section on the "new religious spirit," the argument constructed by this late minister of the church depends not at all upon religious conviction, except perhaps in a political optimism which might only be sustained by faith. In fact, Irvine never returned to the church in his former capacity; *The Farmers In Politics* would appear to mark a transition in his own thought towards a more materialist and secular form. In this he only anticipated the eventual movement of the Canadian Left away from its social gospel origins.[20]

The book begins with a vivid, if perhaps somewhat overexcited, depiction of the new age rising irresistably within the bosom of the old. Old values are crumbling; new values take their place. Profit is replaced by morality, competition by co-operation, individualism by the co-operative commonwealth. Irvine's view of the world is dialectical: competition and co-operation are opposites, yet are united by an evolutionary process which will transcend both in a greater synthesis. There are laws of society, which are natural laws, discoverable by scientific inquiry.

Irvine's analysis of the law of co-operation is an interesting case study in his dialectical method. Co-operation, he argues, arises directly out of the basic human condition of competition. The original state of nature to Irvine was a Hobbesian war of all against all. In order to protect themselves against the constant insecurity of this state, men organized themselves into tribes. Paradoxically, this development both encouraged co-operation within the tribe, while organizing and intensifying competition with other tribes, through warfare. Similarly, the nation state offered wider scope for collective action, yet had at the same time raised warfare to new levels of savagery. The free market economy saw similar developments: capitalists abolished competition among themselves, by mergers, monopolies and cartels which organized and rigged the market. Yet this allowed them greater scope for carrying on economic warfare against other groups, such as farmers and labour. When the latter groups organized themselves, greater group co-operation would lead to more intense conflict between economic interests. The thrust of this analysis is that an inevitable logic leads to higher and higher stages of co-operation precisely in order to carry on competition at a more effective level. Yet this process can end only when competition digs its own grave by organizing itself out of existence. Self-interest is thus a motor force which ultimately transcends itself. The argument is an ingenious, if sketchy, extension of Hobbes within an Hegelian developmental framework. Religion and morality, *pace* Allen, have nothing to do with the immanence of the new and better society, which, paradoxically, arises out of the basest of material motives.

To Irvine, political forms are the reflection of underlying economic realities. "Government forms," he wrote, "are no more permanent than industrial or educational forms. Governments take their forms from the economic basis upon which they rest, and for which they function." (p. 55) The governmental form being rendered obsolete by the rise of new forces from below is the two-party system. Originally based on the economic struggle between the decaying feudal aristocracy and the rising bourgeoisie, the Conservative and Liberal parties, particularly in the Canadian context, no longer reflect any real balance of forces, but linger on as a "fetish," uniting those at the top through the linkage of control by campaign fundings, and manipulation of opinion, while dividing those at the bottom along irrelevant partisan lines. Nor does this mystifying party system have any basis in individual psychology: every person has liberal and conservative characteristics, inextricably mingled together. The point is that the economic organization of workers and farmers offers an alternative: occupational representation along class lines. Pointing to concrete signs of the decay of the two-party system and the emergence of new group representation in provincial legislatures, Irvine argued that his alternative model was a fact, not a theory.

Party organization is itself the enemy of democracy, whether the party in question is an old line organization, or one which purports to represent radical ideas. Here Irvine spoke with the authentic accents of the anti-party traditions of the Canadian West: political parties were eastern, business-dominated systems of corruption which smothered regional and class minorities under the device of parliamentary discipline. Irvine would have agreed with Robert Michels' "iron law of oligarchy" as applied to socialist parties attempting to embody egalitarian and democratic principles in their own organization, but Irvine drew a sharp distinction between *party* organization and *economic* organization. In a complex, class-divided capitalist society, the former is inherently anti-democratic, since it mystifies different class interests by lumping them together in evanescent electoral coalitions. Economic organization based on productive units is inherently democratic, on the other hand, since it directly expresses true *self-interest*, unmediated by shifting secondary associations.

There is an apparent paradox in this argument: if democracy means only the expression of self-interest, how can collective decisions emerge from the clash of various self-interests? Irvine's solution is by no means entirely satisfactory, but neither is it as simplistic or naive as some of the attacks on the party system which had appeared at that time, or which have come forward more recently in Canadian history. Irvine begins by redefining democracy: "a very popular term—chiefly because nobody knows what is meant by it." The political actions of the masses have hitherto been those of the mob, a rabble of individuals manipulated by the ruling class. Universal adult suffrage does not in itself indicate democracy:

A mob is a mob whether it is engaged in a lynching operation, or in throwing little pieces of paper into a ballot box. A mob might be defined as a number of people acting on an idea which does not belong to them; whereas a number of people acting on an idea, which, by a synthetic process involving a compounding of the different ideas of all the individuals concerned, is theirs, would be a democracy. (p. 152)

Democracy must start at the lowest level, which is that of the productive unit. Group solidarity and co-operation in the workplace is the school of democracy, for it is here that individual self-interests are organized around the common economic goals, where each man's interests are advanced by collective action with those engaged in similar productive activity. Political *ideas* are merely part of the superstructure, and thus transitory. Economic *interests* are primary, and form an enduring basis for collective human activity. Interests lead to organization, and ideas emerge from the latter. To reverse this process is to mystify the natural order of things, which is precisely what top-down "non-class" parties have done, by imposing political ideologies from without—on behalf of ruling class interests, of course. The Farmers' Platform[21] is, on the other hand, a genuinely democratic production, in that it emerged from democratic groups of farmers organized around their economic interests. "It is," Irvine affirms, "the first democratic utterance of political significance to be heard in Dominion politics." (pp. 168-9)

Having established democracy at the level of the productive unit, Irvine still faces the problem of how collective political decisions can emerge from the competition of these divergent economic interests. Syndicalism might build on the basis suggested by Irvine: a revolutionary overthrow of capitalism through direct mass action, with the economic organizations of the masses forming the nucleus of the organization of the post-revolutionary society. Irvine, however, rejects Bakunin and the revolutionary anarchist tradition. He similarly rejects Marx, whom he identifies with Russian Bolshevism, as representing the opposite extreme to anarchism: state bureaucratic control by a revolutionary elite. Instead Irvine looks to the British school of evolutionary guild socialism as a middle way. His rejection of revolutionary socialist models does not rest primarily on moral grounds, or on liberal scruples, but rather on a materialist assumption about the organization of society. In developing this assumption, Irvine demonstrates that his guild socialism is more than merely a derivative idea grafted onto the Canadian system, but an idea of some originality.

Class and class interests are the result of the division of labour in society. This division of labour is along functional lines and will exist irrespective of the form of organization of the society. A socialist society will continue to divide people into functional groups, just as capitalist society does. While this might appear to indicate the irreducibility of group interests and thus of group conflict, Irvine assumes that the functional division of labour represents a potential harmony of interests through mutual dependency for the exchange of goods and services. Society should be like an efficient factory, in which the myriad of individual tasks are co-ordinated within a complex, yet natural, organizational blend which would be based not on hierarchy and authority, as in capitalist industry, but on co-operation, the enlightened form of self-interest. This is, to put it mildly, a somewhat heroic assumption, involving as it does the transposition of the Platonic conception of justice (each unit of the community performing its proper function in co-operation with others) to an industrialized capitalist economy without, moreover, any place for a caste of philosopher-kings to oversee the spiritual health of the Republic. The Platonic analogy is, however, merely superficial, despite Irvine's insistence on the harmonic basis of the just social order. For in Irvine's basically Hobbesian universe, harmony emerges precisely out of an intensification of self-interest and of class conflict. Only when each productive group openly recognizes its own group interests as primary, and organizes itself politically around this self-interest, will the true basis for social co-operation be laid bare. When all the cards are on the table, when there is an honest recognition of class selfishness as the motive power of human action, but with *all* classes represented openly and frankly, then the Platonic conception of justice can be effected, as each group recognizes its dependency on every other through a rational calculus of enlightened self-interest. For this organic stage of co-operation to be achieved, it is necessary that all intermediary associations between the economic group and the decision-making process be eliminated, particularly political parties, which will be replaced by functional representatives, acting as direct delegates of their economic constituents.

An apparent weakness in this group government doctrine, especially as handled by some of the farmer philosophers themselves, such as Henry Wise Wood, was its confusion of classes with producer groups. Indeed, C. B. Macpherson makes this a central part of his critique of the social theory of the United Farmers of Alberta.[22] For Macpherson, this confirmed his thesis concerning the petit bourgeois nature of the Alberta farmers' ideology, in its characteristic refusal to see the class basis of capitalist society deriving from the petite bourgeoisie's own ambiguous class position between capital and labour. Macpherson is undoubtedly correct in his critique of the broad position of the farmers' movement as a whole, and Irvine himself did fall into the same confusion. Yet, perhaps because he was an outsider, or because of his education in European labour-socialist thought, it is interesting to note that Irving at the same time pointed to an intriguing and imaginative way out of the dilemma he himself had set.

The dilemma, briefly, is this: class solidarity cuts across the lines of division among producer groups, and *vice versa*. A class conscious working class will unite miners, transport workers, and steel workers around their common position as wage labour in the employ of owners. Producer consciousness will on the other hand unite the workers around their own industrial interests, which may divide them, as *workers*; that is, higher wages for transport workers may reduce the return to miners by raising the cost of the product. Higher wages to miners may increase the cost of steel production and thus reduce the capacity of steel workers to gain wage increases. Producer groups, moreover, may well involve inter-class solidarity along industrial lines; owners, managers and workers function together in a corporatist arrangement against other industries. There is indeed little in the group government doctrine as expounded by the farmers to indicate whether ownership and management of productive units were to remain unchanged under the new governmental arrangements. It was not an issue about which farmers concerned themselves, since it was a problem with which they themselves did not have to deal, given the family farm as the basic unit of agricultural production. It is also a question about which Irvine, as a socialist, is rather pointedly vague, perhaps evasive. At one point in *The Farmers in Politics*, he argues in good corporatist fashion as follows:

> Reformers,to be successful, must be able to give the positive presentation of their case. Instead of saying: "Upset the government," "Down with capital," "To hell with the system," etc., they must say: "We come to fulfill the highest functions of these." Capital must be used to greater advantage for the common good; it must be made to serve. Capitalists will not be destroyed; they will be called to the higher service of managing capital for national well-being. . . . (pp. 96-7)

Similarly, two years later in the House of Commons, Irvine refused to be drawn into a debate over the merits of public versus private ownership of railways, saying that he was more interested in *how* an enterprise was run than in *who* owned it, and then called for co-operative management of the CNR to include representatives of the workers as well as the public.[23] At another point in his book, when he looks to the shape of the new society which will "replace capitalism," he goes on to talk about the right of self-determination of classes: "All classes must be recognized. The real classes are the industrial groups, and of these there are as many as there are industries." (p. 232)

These statements would seem to preclude altogether any Marxist conception of class as deriving from the basic ownership of the means of production. Yet Irvine is not at all unaware of this conception, and indeed falls into a loose Marxist framework on occasion. There is an inconsistency here which no amount of gloss will cover. Irvine's mind was, above all, eclectic: caught between his labour-socialist background on the one hand, and his advocacy of the farmers' movement on the other, he found himself caught between two contradictory conceptions of the social and economic order. He does not resolve the contradiction, by any means, but his tentative solution is certainly original.

When he falls back into what I would call a loose Marxist conceptual framework, he sees the modern capitalist economy divided into three basic classes: the capitalists, the workers, and a middle group of independent producers, of which the farmers are the chief representative. The conflict between capital and labour, when put into these naked terms—shorn of the industrial identifications which otherwise obscure this fundamental division—seems on the face of it, antagonistic and irresolvable. Both sides had organized, and the rise of labour militancy had already manifested itself in Canada through the Winnipeg General Strike, as it previously had on a larger scale in other countries. The stage was set for a terrible struggle. Here Irvine departs from Marx, although in curious parallel with him. Where Marx saw the proletariat as the "universal class" which, since it had no lower class left to exploit, could only emancipate mankind from class exploitation by overthrowing its own exploiters, so too, Irvine looked to a "universal class." In Canada, this was not the proletariat, but the farmers. They are the last to organize themselves, and they are also the most important class, in terms of numbers. The farmers, as a "universal class," have a special mission to end class rule. "The farmers alone," Irvine writes, "have discovered the higher law of co-operation. While other groups exist by co-operation, they do not see that co-operation must be applied between competing groups." In a remarkable synthesis of Marxism and agrarian guild socialism, Irvine argues that:

The farmers are in a position to do great national service, not only because they woke to consciousness in the midst of a changing world, but also because their aims are synthetic. Although fathered by oppression, the farmers' movement has escaped that bitterness of feeling against capital, and that extreme rashness both of expression and action, so characteristic of labor. *The farmer, in reality, combines in his own profession, the two antagonists. He is both capitalist and laborer.* He knows that production is not furthered when war is going on between the two. He sees, also the hopeless deadlock between organized capital and organized labor in the world of industry and commerce, and is thus led to the discovery of co-operation as the synthesis without which progress cannot be made. In this way the United Farmers have become the apostles of co-operation: they have captured the imagination of the nation by combining true radicalism with scientific moderation, and it is safe to say that they are the most hopeful factor in Canadian national life to-day. [emphasis added]. (pp. 101-2)

Thus the farmers will act as the special class with an historic mission to reconcile the antagonistic class forces of capital and labour. Marx's universal class, the proletariat, would abolish class conflict by abolishing class divisions. Irvine's universal class would abolish class conflict by instituting co-operation between continuing classes.[24] Marx's ultimate stage of communism would also be one in which co-operation was the basic form of economic relationship, but this co-operation is an end, not a means. To Irvine, co-operation is both end and means.

This then was Irvine's considered statement of political philosophy at the high tide of the farmers' mobilization amid the radical aura of post-war agitation—but before the returns had begun to come in on the effectiveness of these ideas and of the political movement as a whole. It is, as Irvine himself was aware, an untidy, unfinished work: but it reflected an untidy, unfinished political movement. The freshness of mind, the optimism, the vigor and good humour with which the argument is pursued, make it a work typical of that rather innocent moment of radical confidence—soon to be drained and dissipated by the unexpected strength and tenacity of the old order and its old values. As Nellie McClung later recalled of the feminist movement, its militants went "singing up the hill." For all their sunny optimism, many were to find that the top of the hill was a graveyard for their radical dreams.

Even in *The Farmers in Politics*, the seeds of self-destruction can be discerned. The banking of radical capital on the farmers was a dangerous gamble, for all of Irvine's assiduous theoretical efforts to prove the contrary. The obsession of the analysis with political forms, to the exclusion of any probing of the economic structures, meant that most of the radical energy of the movement was to be directed toward the attack on the party system and the establishment of group government. How this was to be achieved in the face of the British system of cabinet government and party discipline, especially when the structure of group government had been left so vague as to be merely utopian, was not at all clear. Finally, the contradiction between the producer group theory and a more conventional class analysis was left largely unresolved, despite Irvine's ingenious attempt to link the two through the universal class role of the farmers.

In Ontario, Alberta, and Manitoba, farmer parties assumed office in traditional manner, with cabinet posts reserved for their supporters—which in Ontario included some Labour members. In these legislatures, cabinet government functioned more or less as it always had. In the federal House of Commons, the large Progressive contingent refused to act as the official opposition, thus allowing the shattered Tory forces to maintain appearances, and perpetuate the two-party image of Parliament. Irvine's attempt to alter parliamentary procedure to allow the government to hold a confidence vote after losing on a substantive issue in the House, and to carry on if that confidence motion passed—a device to break party discipline and make the House of Commons more like the American Congress—failed when the combined forces of the Liberal and Conservative parties defeated his proposal. An attempt to change the electoral system to Proportional Representation, moved by Irvine's Ontario Progressive colleague and friend, W. C. Good, also failed, thus dashing hopes of altering the voting system along lines more favourable to functional, or group, representation.[25] Interestingly, in the closing section of *The Farmers in Politics*, Irvine pessimistically contemplated the consequences if his ideas failed of achievement. "There is only one constitutional alternative to group representation in parliament," he admitted, "and that is to continue the party system." If the farmers choose the path "which leads to party government," "little of value will be attained, and the whole democratic fight will have to be fought over again." In a rare show of conservatism, Irvine then avers that "it may take thousands of years to accomplish co-operation." If the people are not ready for group government, then "civilization will have to wait until they are." (pp. 223, 226)

Group government did fail to find realization, and in its place the farmers' movement had no alternative political plan, and an embarrasing void where a searching economic analysis of capitalist society should have been. Worse yet, it quickly became apparent that many of the Progressive leaders, including the national leader, T. A. Crerar, were merely Liberals in disguise, more than ready to return to the fold. The story of how Mackenzie King swallowed the Progessives one by one is edifying in terms of political shrewdness, although not in terms of radical ideals.

Irvine, as a Labour member, co-operated where possible with the Progressive members, but grew increasingly critical of their failure to follow through on their promise. Eventually, he and his leader, J. S. Woodsworth ("I wish to state", Irvine cheerfully informed the House, "that the honorable member for Centre Winnipeg is the leader of the Labour group—and I am the group"[26]) formed the "Ginger group" with the more advanced Progressive members, a group which became the nucleus of the CCF party in the 1930s. But the hopes of the immediate postwar period, and the exalted historical role assigned to the farmers by Irvine in his book, dribbled unheroically away. In 1925, Irvine publicly put his feelings on record in parliament:

> I regret to find no bright hopes in the Progressive party so far as labour is concerned, and I abandon my hopes of it very reluctantly. Many forward-looking people to-day see in the Progressive party as it now is a fitting epitaph for the tomb of a lost opportunity.... (T)he flood time has passed, the ebb has now set in, and the Progressive party is now grasping and wriggling like a fish left stranded on the beach before the receding tide. There I will leave them.... [26]

To Irvine the failure was of the Progressives, not of the concept of group government itself. As late as 1929, Irvine published another book, *Co-operative Government*, in which the case for group organization of government was restated in even more far-reaching terms, this time involving the elimination of constituency voting, with replacement by a quota system of a fixed number of representatives from each group, no matter how small. The number of representatives was to be determined by "the value of the service rendered to the community, and not the numbers employed.... Function and numbers, rather than territory and numbers, should be the factors considered."[27] This was travelling pretty far down the road to corporatism. Indeed, there might appear to be much in common with the liberal corporatism of Mackenzie King's *Industry and Humanity*, which Irvine was given to citing now and again. But King did nothing whatever to establish the ideas he had so broadly and sententiously enunciated in his book, despite his position in national office, while Irvine was a powerless backbencher well outside the mainstream of Canadian politics. It is perhaps not surprising that Irvine was particularly bitter towards the Liberals and their leader, who was the master of co-optation of left wing dissent.

As a member of Parliament, Irvine was best described as the proverbial gadfly. He made his maiden speech in the House on the eighth day of his first session; instead of praising the beauties of his riding in the traditional manner, he began by citing Hegel, and then launched into an attack on the party system and the banking system.[28] From then on, Irvine was regularly heard on all sorts of issues. The only times when he was silent were when he was defeated and out of Parliament, as he was in 1925, from 1935 to 1945, and after 1949. Gerrymandered out of a seat, Irvine could come bouncing back in again from elsewhere. Over the years he represented three different constituencies, including one in British Columbia. Although he had few illusions about the usefulness of Parliament, it did give him a job, and a forum for his eloquence and fertile political imagination. His name became associated not only with lost causes, such as group government, but with liberal ideas in advance of their time, such as the abolition of capital punishment and the reform of the divorce laws to put wives on an equal footing with husbands.[29] Irvine, along with Woodsworth and A. A. Heaps also acted as a three-man pressure group to draw public attention to labour issues and the grievances of the working class. The most spectacular example in the early 1920s was the crisis in the Cape Breton coal mines, when the British Empire Steel Corporation slashed the wages of the workers by a third, while the Liberal provincial and federal governments acted to jail union leaders and support the company.[30] On issues such as this, Irvine was unfailingly on the side of the workers.

One issue with which Irvine forcefully associated himself during the 1920s, not without ambiguity to his ideological position, was advocacy of Social Credit. In lieu of either a Marxist critique of the structure of capitalism or of a fully developed social-democratic critique of the economic practice of capitalism, Irvine's economic thought was somewhat eccentric. Although he was never a monomaniac on the subject, as the true believers later proved to be, Irvine did place considerable weight on the views of monetary reformists, particularly those of Major C. H. Douglas, founder of the Social Credit movement in England. Premissed on an "underconsumptionist" theory of business cycles, Irvine's views ran strongly towards social control of the credit system and the provision of sufficient purchasing power in the hands of the people to maintain effective demand for the goods and services produced. Production was not itself the problem and could, Irvine believed, be carried out effectively either under capitalism or socialism. The real problem was distribution, and the source of the problem was the *money* economy. Instead of being a social or collective service, geared to the common good, the financial system had, under capitalism, fallen under the control of finance capital, in the form of socially irresponsible bankers. Following Hobson and Lenin, Irvine further suggested that the growing power of finance capital, along with the underconsumption endemic to industrial societies, had generated imperialism in search of markets for surplus goods and investment, and thus exacerbated the chance of war through inter-imperialist rivalry.[31]

Social Credit, in its broadest and most basic meaning, that of the ability of a nation to use credit on the assumption of future economic growth returning a social surplus is, as Robin Neill has pointed out, a developmental strategy for a new nation differing from the National Policy strategy only in its "institutional instruments and the implications for the distribution of the results of accumulation"; as such, it had deep and indigenous roots in Canada extending back well into the nineteenth century.[32] Irvine succeeded in referring a motion to investigate the credit system to the House Committee on Banking and Commerce in 1923. Irvine, working closely with W. C. Good, had a number of witnesses called to present unorthodox views. George Bevington, an Alberta farmer of proto-Social Credit views, testified at some length, and was later followed by Major Douglas himself, who came from England for the occasion. Also called were leading bankers and academic economists. The hearings thus present a valuable insight into the state of thinking in the country on monetary questions at this time. It must be said that much of the left wing attack on the bankers and orthodox economists reads very well from a respectable post-Keynesian perspective. Indeed, much of what appeared to be radical and crankish notions to the conventional wisdom of the early 1920s seems to be merely unexceptionable good sense today. The notion of government script replacing private bank notes as sole legal tender, the idea of a central bank, the demystification of the gold standard, the recognition that banks create credit through loans and that the actual amount of currency in circulation is a small percentage of the total money supply—all these have become the conventional wisdom of a later day. Irvine's sharp intelligence demonstrated itself time and again when confronting the pillars of finance or of academe. One of the barons of Bay Street, Sir John Aird, was reduced to pleading that "we do not want theories introduced into banking. If you get into theories you are on dangerous ground."[33] It might also be pointed out that Irvine's thesis of underconsumption, although deficient in itself, did suggest what one mainstream economist has called the "characteristic radical groping towards the formulation of important economic principles and concepts," including a "close Canadian approach to a Keynesian basis for fiscal policy. . . . one of the earliest statements of principle to capture the spirit, if not the letter, of the 'national employment budget,' the concept of the 'gross national product,' and the role of the government in the achievement of high and stable levels of employment and income."[34]

Unfortunately for Irvine, despite his avowals that so far as the Douglas system of Social Credit went he was "merely a student of the subject. . . . not a propagandist,"[35] the popularizing of Social Credit was an activity with disastrous and ironic consequences for an Alberta socialist. Social Credit was an idea which had immense scope for organizing the western farmers in a manner which could only spell trouble for convinced socialists. To the farmers, the major villains of capitalism, as manifested in everyday life, were the banks and loan companies, the distant manipulators who foreclosed on mortgages, and charged fixed interest without regard to the very unfixed distribution of rainfall, temperature, and world price for wheat. The bankers were the fly in the ointment of the yeoman republic of independent producers, a constant reminder that the farmers' property was not really theirs, that the fruits of their labour were already expropriated in advance. When the Depression deepened this already difficult situation, the Social Credit promise of money to each individual in the form of Social Credit script had just the right touch of demagogic simplicity to sweep the electorate. Finally, Social Credit offered a peculiar but devastating mixture of radicalism and conservatism: a single, simple adjustment theory of what had gone wrong, which offered the easy comfort of cultural continuity and the familiar moral verities along with a painless reform which would affect only an unpopular lot of bankers mainly resident in distant Toronto and Montreal. The evangelical fundamentalism of Bible Bill Aberhart in the charismatic campaign which swept Alberta in 1935 was in a sense a parody of the social gospel which had given such impetus to the earlier socialist and reform movement at the end of the war.[36] In another sense, it was merely a *reductio ad absurdem* of the weaknesses of the social gospel and the reformism based upon it. Irvine's views in the 1920s *could* issue in Social Credit, just as the ideology of the farmers' movement always bore that possibility. In the event, the vicissitudes of time and circumstance threw up Social Credit in Alberta, and a social democratic farmer-labour party in Saskatchewan. Irvine, who as late as the eve of the Socred sweep in Alberta was moving a Social Credit amendment to the federal budget,[37] was horrified at the reality of the monster brought to birth under the name of Social Credit—"the most extraordinary will-o'-the-wisp that has ever been projected into political discussion in this country," as he was later to characterize it.[38] It was particularly ironic that it should be in Alberta, Irvine's own province, where Social Credit took hold as an alternative to agrarian socialism. From 1935 on, Irvine was fated to continue his CCF activities in an arid political wilderness, while his chosen political vehicle went from success to success in the province next door.

With the demise of the Progressives and the dissipation of the thrust behind the farmers' movement, the rationale of the group government concept was lost. Not all the adherents of the idea gave it up—as late as 1933 W. C. Good was continuing to advocate the old concept in a memorable exchange with Frank Underhill in the *Canadian Forum*[39]—but Irvine, with his characteristic openmindedness and flexibility, appears to have abandoned interest in the idea. Despite his earlier strictures about the corrupting influence even of reform or radical political parties on their members, if they were to be organized as electoral parties, he threw himself with great gusto and dedication into the task of building a farmer-labour political party in the 1930s. The famous meeting of left wing MP's which set in motion the founding of the CCF party was held in Irvine's office in the House of Commons. Of course, the new party, although clearly organized as an electoral party attempting to attract the support of various groups, across occupational lines, and quite willing to employ such heretical devices as party discipline in the legislature, was not quite what the old line parties had been. There is no doubt that from the beginning the CCF was more democratic in its structure and more principled in its approach to the electorate. In Walter D. Young's terms, it was both a political party seeking electoral success and a social movement seeking to change the moral climate of the country. In its latter guise it did continue to bear some of the features of its antecedents of the 1920s. As the movement aspect diminished while the party aspect waxed stronger, the old voices of anti-partyism could still be heard—and sometimes among them was William Irvine.[40] Yet it had become clear to him that however much the party system might offend his sensibilities, the only possible way for the workers and farmers to fight back against class oppression was to organize themselves as a political party and to make compromises in their own organization for the greater good of the idea of socialism. Irvine was a realist. Ends and means could not always match perfectly, in an imperfect world. When they did not, it might be necessary to adopt means that were not entirely consonant with the ultimate goals. Party organization and party discipline were among such means.

An example of how far this thinking had changed is to be found in a play which he wrote in the mid-1930s, *The Brains We Trust*, which was performed in Toronto and Edmonton.[41] It is a satire of the 1935 election, with a Socialist party filled with well-meaning idealists and led by a saintly figure obviously representing J. S. Woodsworth. In this play there is an interesting section in which socialist strategy is discussed by the new party's leaders. The party, it appears, is beset by moderates who wish to disguise socialism as something acceptable to non-socialists, to talk in populist terms which people understand, while avoiding Marxist concepts such as "surplus value" and "economic determinism." The issue is resolved on the basis that socialism must be based on a movement, not a political party— votes must be *real*. Socialism cannot be won without winning elections, but elections can be won while socialism is lost. Irvine clearly was trying to resolve the contradiction between his old and new view of political organization.

His devotion to the new party cannot be questioned. Defeated in 1935, and out of Parliament for the ten years following, Irvine did not seek employment which might offer him some economic security, but instead turned his attention full time to organizing and propagandizing for the CCF, on a salary so intermittent and low that his personal finances were wrecked. That his activities were centered in Alberta, where Social Credit had virtually pre-empted the entire potential vote for the CCF, is further confirmation of his dedication against depressing odds. In 1940 he was reduced to begging national headquarters for a loan of a few hundred dollars so that he could build himself a modest home in which to live. "If I had a place of my own", he wrote David Lewis,

> however small and humble, it would give me a sense of secu-
> rity which I now lack and besides I could get along on a very
> small income if I didn't have to pay rent ... it won't be very
> long until I will be unable to carry on the rough and tumble
> of organization work. Then what? The thought of an old man
> pennyless, and in poverty is not a good thought to live with
> during a sleepless night.[42]

Lewis tried unsuccessfully to raise the money, and Irvine's problems grew worse. Somehow he carried on, and in 1945 managed to get himself back in Parliament for the last time. The house was built, and Irvine and his wife lived in it until his death.

The idea of socialism to which Irvine showed such selfless dedication was, to the end, an eclectic, indefinable blend of British Labourite thought, North American populism, agrarian radicalism, anarcho-syndicalism, and quasi-Marxist concepts.[43] He picked up considerable intellectual baggage along the way, and most of it showed. It would be futile to attempt to neatly categorize this astonishing collection of ideas under any convenient lable. There is no doubt that he remained a social democrat, in the sense that he never believed that revolution was necessary nor that a dictatorship of the proletariat was either a sensible or desirable concept. Marx provided some good ideas to Irvine, but never a comprehensive world view which would exclude any other. On the other hand, his fierce devotion to the underdogs of society, his congenital open-mindness, and his constant radical questioning of accepted verities, all tended to place him on the left wing of the CCF. He was, in the end, a party man in the best sense, of loyalty and work, but he remained his own man in terms of ideas and principles.

This obstinate individualism drew him into great difficulties with the party in his last years. Irvine was not stampeded by the

Cold War atmosphere of the 1950s to change his lifelong aversion towards armaments, militarism, and "patriotism" as the last refuge of scoundrels. Although, unlike Woodsworth, he was not a pacifist, he maintained throughout his life a deep distrust of those who wished to project political conflict away from the internal class issues of capitalist society and onto foreign "enemies." Moreover, the specific ideological thrust of the Cold War, the mobilization of class solidarity under capitalism against the "menace" of communism, was correctly perceived by Irvine as a blow against progressive forces throughout western society. The mindless celebration of "our way of life" along with the hysterical assault on anything or anyone considered radical could only redound against a social democratic party, however moderate its policies might be in reality. It was thus with increasing misgivings that Irvine watched the CCF eagerly line up behind the Cold War bandwagon. Nor were these foreign policy developments entirely unconnected to the rightward drift of party policy as a whole throughout the 1950's. In 1956 the party replaced the Regina Manifesto, the original platform of 1933 which had called for the eradication of capitalism, with the Winnipeg Declaration which scarcely mentioned public ownership and expressly recognized a place for private enterprise. Irvine was not happy: "we were born in the manger of poverty and the old capitalists are still the same."[44] To Irvine the domestic and foreign policy trends were clearly linked. The Cold War rearmament had, he argued, prevented the reversion of the capitalist economies to large-scale unemployment and depression following the end of the Second World War. Irvine's old underconsumptionist theory of business cycles was thus maintained, but the Western world's artificial and dangerous answer to the problem left the basic question unresolved: if the instability of capitalism could only be evaded by preparations for war, a radical solution to the problem became even more urgent than before, now that atomic weapons raised the spectre of the destruction of the planet itself. The challenge was for social democracy to develop a position distinct from either capitalism or communism. Irvine's logic was simple: "social democracy either has a position which is different from both, or it has no position at all."[45]

That he may have entertained despairing thoughts that social democracy has indeed no position left is one possible interpretation of his last significant political actions: visits to the Soviet Union and the People's Republic of China. Irvine's visit to the

Soviet Union in 1956 along with some fellow Alberta CCFers, nearly got him expelled from the party to which he had devoted his life. Irvine had never been a doctrinaire opponent of the Canadian Communist party, unlike some CCFers. On occasion he had co-operated with the Communists in joint ventures or common fronts, but this was for tactical reasons.[46] On the other hand, he wished to see the Soviet Union for himself, rather than through the eyes of the Western media. When the Tass news agency quoted Irvine as commenting favourably on the existence of economic democracy in the Soviet Union, the CCF executive reacted violently. A press release under the signature of the national leader, M. J. Coldwell, told the Canadian press that "on his return to Canada, Mr. Irvine will be queried with respect to any statement he may actually have made. If there is any suggestion at all of approval by him of a one-party dictatorship, it will be immediately and completely repudiated by the CCF."[47] Irvine's position as Alberta party president appeared to implicate the party in a pro-Communist stance from which it had been trying desperately to distance itself, in the face of right wing, anti-CCF propaganda. Irvine was, however, unrepentant upon his return. Although his expulsion from the party was seriously discussed on an informal level, it was thought wiser to leave him alone, not only because in the words of the national secretary, "We must recognize the very special place which he has in our movement, the long years that he has contributed to and sacrificed for it and the fact that it would break his heart to be tossed out at this late stage in his life by those with whom he worked so long," but also because he still had, "even in spite of his recent folly, a tremendous number of followers in the movement": his expulsion would cause a "major schism."[48]

Irvine had been genuinely impressed with what he had seen in the Soviet Union, and had no intention of remaining silent on the subject, despite complaints from party colleagues that he was making speeches "indistinguishable from those of Tim Buck." Despite the impression of naivety which he gave to anti-communist CCFers, Irvine was not unaware of the "warts" in the Soviet way of life. When he published a book about his Russian experiences in 1958, *Live or Die With Russia*, he had made a conscious decision that anti-Soviet propaganda had to be counteracted, and that the "warts" would not be emphasized.[49] It was above all his concern for coexistence and peace which animated this decision, yet it is difficult to read this book without sensing an uncritical quality in Irvine's enthusiastic description of his guided tour. Like a long line of Western radicals, such as the Webbs and Lincoln Steffins, Irvine's good will somewhat outran his critical faculty when confronted with the Soviet system. The Soviets were sufficiently impressed with the book to have it translated into Russian. In any event, the Alberta CCF executive supported him, and some of its members involved themselves in the Stockholm Peace Congress, labelled a Communist front by the national party. Unbowed, Irvine then went on a trip to Mao's China which, if anything, was considered even farther beyond the pale at this time. In 1961, a year before his death, yet another book was published, *The Twain Shall Meet*, written by Irvine and some of his companions on his China visit. As the title indicates, it was an appeal for understanding between east and west.[50]

In 1961, Irvine was a delegate to the founding convention of the New Democratic party, the successor to the CCF, and then helped organize the Alberta NDP.[51] His party loyalty remained to the end. He died in 1962, completing a political career as interesting and as colourful as any in Canadian history.

Is there any thread of unity in this long and eclectic career? *The Farmers in Politics* provides a clue to the underlying continuity not only of Irvine's thought but of the social democratic left in this century. Any attempt to root Canadian socialism in the reality of the Canadian political economy necessitated the recognition of the crucial importance of the rural population and way of life. That it was the farmers who were in the vanguard of the first major class confrontation with capitalism in this century set the tone of ideological conflict for generations to come. Irvine, perhaps more than any other political figure, attempted to work out the implications of this for radical politics. In drawing the underlying assumptions of the farmers as a class force out into the scrutiny of rational analysis, he also demonstrated the ambiguities and contradictions inherent in farmer-labour alliances. Yet his tenacious insistence upon the cardinal importance of this class alliance as a progressive force is equally important. In other countries, the petit bourgeois rural population has sometimes turned into a bulwark of reaction, or even the electoral backbone of fascism (as in Weimar Germany). Social Credit did exhibit some of these tendencies, but even it never became authoritarian or anti-semitic on the European scale. On the other hand, agrarian socialism took firm hold in Saskatchewan, and the western farmer has always been a factor of significance in both the CCF and the NDP. That the farmers have continued to act as a radical force on occasion—although not always, by any means—has been of particular importance to the Canadian Left. On the other hand, the influence of the farmers on the social democratic party has no doubt contributed to its populist, non-Marxist ideological bent, and its petit bourgeois political instincts so decried by Marxist critics, such as the now defunct Waffle wing of the party expelled in the early 1970s.

In the late twentieth century, the independent commodity producers have declined to the point of near extinction as a significant factor in the Canadian economy. Preservation of the family farm and the rural way of life in the face of corporate farming and agribusiness seems to be a losing battle. Despite its predominantly labour foundations, the NDP continues to maintain its old traditions by supporting the disappearing family farm against the Liberal celebration of consolidation and "modernization," and still gains electoral support in rural Saskatchewan and other prairie locations. The National Farmers Union maintains the radical—and non-partisan—traditions of agrarian protest with such tactics as product boycotts and tractor blockades of highways. It is, however, obvious that the major focus of class conflict has shifted toward the industrial sector and the confrontation between organized labour and corporate capitalism. In this sense, Irvine's book is a summation of an era which has now largely passed. It is none the less important for it is a vivid and lively statement of a thoughtful political figure from a crucial era in the development of radical thought and practice in this country.

Acknowledgements

I should like to thank the following persons for assistance in the preparation of this introduction. Professor Tony Mardiros of the University of Alberta was kind enough to provide me with information on Irvine's life and works: I look forward to the biography of Irvine which he is currently writing. Mr. Robin Sears, National Director of the New Democratic Party, allowed me to examine the CCF Records in the Public Archives of Canada. Finally the staff of the latter institution, particularly Mr. Ian McClymont, were as helpful as always to researchers.

Notes to Carleton Library Edition

1. Perhaps the classic statement of this liberal pluralist view is to be found in J. A. Corry and J. E. Hodgetts, *Democratic Government and Politics* (Toronto, 1969).
2. Foreign observers of Canadian politics have been quick to note the unprincipled and even sordid nature of Political bargaining. See André Siegfried, *The Race Question in Canada* (1907; new edition: Toronto: Carleton Library No. 29, 1964), and Viscount Bryce, *Canada, an Actual Democracy* (Toronto, 1921).
3. Gustavus Myers, *History of Canadian Wealth* (1914; new edition: Toronto, 1972) is the earliest example of this genre. More recent examples include R. T. Naylor, *The History of Canadian Business*, 2 vols. (Toronto, 1975); Robert Chodos, *CPR: A Century of Corporate Welfare* (Toronto, 1973); John Deverell, *Falconbridge: Portrait of a Canadian Mining Multinational* (Toronto, 1975); Larry Pratt, *The Tar Sands: Syncrude and the Politics of Oil* (Edmonton, 1976).
4. John Porter, *The Vertical Mosaic* (Toronto, 1965); Wallace Clement, *The Canadian Corporate Elite* (Toronto: Carleton Library No. 89, 1975).
5. For an overview of these developments see D. Drache, "Rediscovering Canadian Political Economy," Paper de-

livered at the Canadian Political Science Association, Annual Meeting, June, 1975.

For an appreciation of the staples model from a mainstream American economic historian, see Glenn Porter, "Recent Trends in Canadian Business and Economic History," *Business History Review*, XLVII: 2 (Summer, 1973), pp. 141-58.

6. There is also a muckraking strain, in the Myers tradition, which is not necessarily Marxist. Naylor's work exhibits this characteristic.

7. W. L. Morton, "Clio in Canada: the Interpretation of Canadian History," *University of Toronto Quarterly*, XV: 3 (April, 1946).

8. I have developed this more fully in "Images of the state in Canada," in Leo Panitch, ed., *The Canadian State: Political Economy and Political Power* (Toronto, 1977), pp. 28-68.

9. The early theorist of colonization, Gibbon Wakefield, made a major point of this relationship. Some of the implications are brought out by Marx in vol. 1 of *Capital*, chapter 33. Haliburton had Sam Slick utter it as an obvious piece of conventional wisdom. T. C. Haliburton, *The Clockmaker, First Series* (Toronto, 1958), p. 27.

10. K. A. H. Buckley and M. C. Urquhart, *Canadian Historical Statistics* (Toronto, 1965).

11. Michael Bliss, *A Living Profit: Studies in the Social History of Canadian Business, 1883-1911* (Toronto, 1974), pp. 117-24.

12. Among the flood of such works, one might single out—in addition to the Irvine book reprinted here—Mackenzie King, *Industry and Humanity* (1918; new edition: Toronto, 1973); Stephen Leacock, *The Unsolved Riddle of Social Justice* (1920: reprinted in Alan Bowker, ed., *The Social Criticism of Stephen Leacock*: Toronto, 1973); W. C. Good, *Production and Taxation in Canada* (Toronto 1919); Salem Bland, *The New Christianity* (1919; new edition: Toronto, 1973).

13. Raymond Williams has recently attempted to reassess the traditional Marxist antipathy to "rural idiocy," *The Country and the City* (London, 1973).

14. I have discussed King's thought at greater length in "The Liberal Corporatist Ideas of Mackenzie King," *Labour/ Le Travailleur*, 2, 1977.

15. Tony Mardiros, "A Man to Remember: William Irvine, 1885-1962," *The Nutcracker*, I: 7 (May, 1975), pp. 4-5. Richard Allen, *The Social Passion: Religious and Social Reform in Canada, 1914-28* (Toronto, 1971), p. 46; Allen interviewed Irvine a year before his death.

16. Tony Mardiros, "William Irvine: Heretic in Politics," *Newest Review*, I: 3 (October, 1975), pp. 1-2. My thanks to Professor Mardiros for supplying me with copies of this article and the one cited in fn. 15, above.

17. Paul F. Sharp, *The Agrarian Revolt in Western Canada: A Survey Showing American Parallels* (1948; reprinted, New York, 1971), pp. 77-104. C. B. Macpherson, *Democracy in Alberta: Social Credit and the Party System* (second edition: Toronto, 1962), pp. 25-6.

18. Macpherson, *op. cit.*, pp. 28-61, offers the most comprehensive and interesting analysis of the social and political theory of the UFA thinkers, including Irvine.

19. Allen, *op. cit.*, p. 208.

20. In 1940, in desperate financial straits, Irvine could still show little enthusiasm for a possible offer of a Unitarian ministry in Ottawa. "My heart is not in the Church as you know," he wrote David Lewis, "but in the CCF. To have to go to the Church for a living would be unfair to the Church and most difficult for me." Public Archives of Canada, CCF Records, v. 97, Irvine to Lewis, no date (1940).

21. The Farmers' Platform was a programme promulgated by the Canadian Council of Agriculture and ratified by the Council's member associations meeting in convention during 1917. It was revised in 1918 under the title of the "New National Policy." L. A. Wood, *A History of Farmers' Movements in Canada: The Origins and Development of Agrarian Protest, 1872-1924* (1924; new edition, Introduction by Foster J. K. Griezic: Toronto, 1975), pp. 345-6.

22. Macpherson, *op. cit.*, pp. 34-8.

23. House of Commons, *Debates*, 1923, pp. 1953-4.

24. It might be noted in passing that the concept of a "universal class" has obsessed numerous other modern political thinkers. To the early liberal thinkers, the bourgeoisie would take on this role; to Hegel, it would be the bureaucrats; to Frantz Fanon, it would be the peasantry and lumpen-proletariat of the Third World. None of

these universal classes, including Marx's proletariat, have ever quite lived up to their advance billing. Irvine was thus only essaying a North American variant of a familiar quest, with as much success as other such attempts.

25. House of Commons, *Debates*, 1923, pp. 208-44; 389-434.

26. *Ibid.*, 1925, p. 1963.

27. *Co-operative Government* (Ottawa: 1929), p. 220. The book begins with a curious foreword by Henry Wise Wood, who states that he knows the author, but has not read the book!

28. House of Commons, *Debates*, 1927, pp. 211-34.

29. Believers in intellectual progress may note sadly that the current debate on retention of capital punishment could have been lifted almost *verbatim* from the debate generated by Irvine's abolitionist bill in 1924, a half century ago. Only the statistical "evidence" has changed; the arguments remain unaltered. See *Debates*, 1924, pp. 1265 ff. Irvine's bill was defeated by a vote of 92 to 29.

30. Kenneth McNaught, *A Prophet in Politics: a Biography of J. S. Woodsworth* (Toronto, 1959), pp. 173-9.

31. Irvine aired his monetary views in a number of forums, one of which was a two volume pamphlet issued in 1924, *Purchasing Power and the World Problem* (Dominion Labor Party, Labor Temple, Calgary). An unpublished graduate paper by David Laycock, "Socialism and Social Credit in the Political Thought of William Irvine" (Department of Political Economy, University of Toronto, 1977), provides a useful inquiry into that question.

32. R. F. Neill, "Social Credit and National Policy in Canada," *Journal of Canadian Studies*, 3 (1968), pp. 3-13.

33. House of Commons, Committee on Banking and Commerce, 1923, *Proceedings and Evidence*, p. 379. The head of the Canadian Bankers Association was similarly stymied by Irvine: "Very difficult to answer. You really might ask a question that Sir Isaac Newton could not answer and I am not Sir Isaac Newton; I am a practical man, that is all. I am not a master of economics." *Ibid*, p. 320.

34. Irving Brecher, *Monetary and Fiscal Thought and Policy in Canada: 1919-1939* (Toronto, 1957) p. 94, and pp. 54-5.

35. Banking and Commerce Committee, *op. cit.*, p. 1047.

36. Macpherson, *op. cit.*; John A. Irving, *The Social Credit*

Movement in Alberta (Toronto, 1959); William E. Mann, *Sect, Cult and Church in Alberta* (Toronto, 1955).

37. Frank Underhill characterized a 1932 speech by Irvine in Toronto in behalf of the new CCF as "pure social credit." Walter D. Young, *The Anatomy of a Party: The National CCF, 1932-61* (Toronto, 1969), p. 34.

38. House of Commons, *Debates*, 1947, p. 1288. The flavour of Irvine's contempt for the religious obscurantism of Social Credit is caught in a letter he wrote to David Lewis concerning Aberhart's successor as premier, Ernest Manning: "Mr. Manning is young, rather well liked and oozes the blood of the lamb over everything. He proved by science, in three lectures on the air, that the whale swallowed Jonah and said that, if the bible had said that Jonah had swallowed the whale, science could prove that too. That is the sort of thing most people like. He will be more popular than 'Abby'." CCF Records v. 74, Irvine to Lewis, June 3, 1943. Irvine's mature views on Social Credit can also be found in a letter to W. C. Good, reprinted in Good's autobiography, *Farmer Citizen* (Toronto, 1958), pp. 215-17.

39. August, 1933. The exchange is reprinted in Good, *op. cit.*, pp. 184-95.

40. Young, *op. cit.*, p. 113.

41. (Toronto: Thomas Nelson and Sons, 1935). He wrote another play the following year, *You Can't Do That*, which was performed in Wetastikiwin (Letter to another from Tony Mardiros, May 23, 1976).

42. CCF Records, v. 97, Irvine to Lewis, August 19, 1940.

43. His 1945 pamphlet, *Is Socialism the Answer? The Intelligent Man's Guide to Basic Democracy* (Winnipeg: Contemporary Publications, 1945), includes a veritable potpourri of influences from American New Dealer Maury Maverick to Karl Marx.

44. Young, *op. cit.*, p. 128.

45. From an unpublished manuscript, "Challenge to the 'Free Private Enterprise' Capitalist Way of Life," CCF Records, v. 300. The manuscript appears to have been written in 1956; that it was not published by the party is scarcely surprising, considering its direct challenge to the views then dominant in the national executive.

46. Young, *op. cit.*, p. 262. Ivan Avakumovic, *The Communist Party in Canada: a History* (Toronto, 1975), pp. 105,

128. In 1943, Irvine assured David Lewis apropos of Communist leader Tim Buck, that "I have never communicated with the gentleman in my life." CCF Records, v. 74, Irvine to Lewis, Nov. 16, 1943.

47. CCF Records, v. 97, CCF Press release, July 19, 1956.

48. *Ibid.*, Lorne Ingle to Elmer Roper, August 9, 1956.

49. *Ibid.*, Roper to Ingle, Sept. 11 and Nov. 3, 1956. Mardiros letter, *op. cit.*

50. Edmonton, 1961. Irvine came off badly with his prediction that "common humanism" would prevent a Sino-Soviet split. He even suggested that the Russian-Chinese alliance would outlive NATO, pp. 132-3.

51. Mardiros, "A Man to Remember," *op. cit.*, p. 5.

The Farmers
in Politics

FOREWORD

BY REV. SALEM G. BLAND, D.D.

Here is a fresh, vigorous, constructive, and Canadian contribution to the solution of our social and political problems.

It is significant and, perhaps, prophetic that it comes from Alberta. Perhaps nowhere in Canada to-day is more interesting and vital thinking going on than in the most western of the three prairie provinces, most western, perhaps, in spirit as in position.

I have followed the career of the author with keen interest since his college days. He has been finding his own way. I believe his dominant passion is devotion to the common people. No one who reads these pages can fail to find sincerity, vigor, and a passion for justice.

Some of the author's *obiter dicta* will not find universal assent, but his analysis of present economic and political conditions in Canada is keen and not easy to refute. The main contribution of the book, however, and, in my judgment, a very considerable one, is the defence of the position the United Farmers of Alberta

seem to be taking in regard to political action—
that the farmers should not try by association
with other progressive and democratic thinkers
to form a national party, but should seek en-
trance into all the legislatures distinctively as a
farmers' party, not, however, to secure class
legislation, but by co-operation with other class
groups to work out policies that would be truly
national. In short, this book is a defence of the
group system in politics as the only method that
is truly democratic. Mr. Irvine is convinced
that the party system is no longer adequate for
the growing complexity of modern society, and
that it is destined to give way to a legislature
and cabinet representative of all considerable
classes in the community and elected by Proportional Representation.

Political organization, in his judgment,
should crystallize not around ideas but around
economic interests, the most substantial and enduring basis of common action. The farmers,
he thinks, should frankly admit they are a class
organization, but not one seeking class domination. Let every group that has a common economic interest similarly organize. Only out of
a conference of such groups can a truly national
policy emerge.

FOREWORD

I question if any more constructive and distinctively Canadian contribution has yet been thrown into the discussion of our national problems.

S. G. BLAND.

Toronto, 1920.

PREFACE

The views put forward in this book are not to be understood as an official pronouncement by, or on behalf of, the farmers' movement. They are rather the earnest and sincere effort of a student of current events to afford some elucidation of pressing questions of economics and politics in Canada at the present time. The farmers' movement has come recently into the limelight, and while it stands, therefore, in little need of introduction, it can only gain by some measure of explanation, not only to the general public, but also to the very many farmer friends who will be glad to be made better acquainted with it.

The farmers' movement is only one phase of the greater democratic movement that is sweeping over the world at this time. Part I. of this volume is an attempt to get a true perspective of that great awakening of the common people which properly forms the background of the farmers' organization. Part II. is devoted to the economic history of the organized farmers, including their political aims, and the efforts put forward by them in their attempt to solve their economic problems.

Considerable criticism has been levelled at the farmers regarding their political aspirations. The charge that the farmers seek to usurp political power for class interests needs to be answered. I have tried to disprove this charge, and have set forth adequate parliamentary representation as the chief aim of the movement's political activity.

I have not aimed at making this a treatise on political economy. Nor, in anything that I have written, do I claim that a final solution is propounded for any of the problems with which I have dealt. There are no such things as final solutions. Every working hypothesis, no matter how admirably it may work, can be no more than a stepping-stone in the advance of human society.

For my effort I would ask that readiness of mind on the part of the reader which will induce diligent inquiry into, and consideration of, the matters taken in hand; so that, if my views do not immediately convince or enlighten, they may at least not be dismissed without consideration. If I succeed in so far arresting attention, my main object, which is to stimulate and intensify public interest, will be gained. I shall feel amply repaid for this attempt if it suggests to better qualified minds and to pens abler than mine the undertaking of a more adequate work.

Were it possible from the platform to reach as many people as may be reached by print, I could, perhaps, say more effectively in that way what I have tried to say here. Ruskin divides all books into two classes—the books of the hour and the books of all time. Inasmuch, however, as any writing dealing with a movement still in process of development can have vitality for only so long as the movement itself is one of current interest, this book has no hope of belonging to Ruskin's latter category, and the writer's fullest hope will be realized if he has succeeded in writing what he acknowledges must necessarily be a book of the hour.

WILLIAM IRVINE.

Calgary, 1920.

CONTENTS

THE FARMERS IN POLITICS

PART II.

THE ORIGIN AND DEVELOPMENT OF THE UNITED FARMERS' MOVEMENT.

PART ONE

THE NEW SOCIAL ORDER IN PERSPECTIVE

CHAPTER I.

THE PROCESS OF READJUSTMENT

Beautiful world of new superber birth, that rises to my
    eyes,
Like a limitless golden cloud, filling the western sky.
Thou Wonder World, yet undefined, unformed—neither
    do I define thee;
How can I pierce the impenetrable blank of the future?
I feel thy ominous greatness, evil as well as good;
I watch thee, advancing, absorbing the present, trans-
    cending the past.
I see thy light lighting and thy shadow shadowing, as if
    the entire globe;
But I do not undertake to define thee—hardly to compre-
    hend thee;
I but thee name—thee prophesy—as now!
                  —WALT WHITMAN.

§1

The New Social Ethics. There are two instruments used largely to-day as aids to human vision: one the microscope, which brings to view the infinitesimal that without its use would remain invisible; the other the telescope which brings into focus that which is beyond the natural limit of sight. Both are equally service-able in the world of science; but they are not interchangeable. The astronomer would be

17

helpless with a microscope, while the biologist would find little use in his laboratory for a telescope.

In approaching the great problems of our civilization, our instruments of vision must be analogous to the telescope. We must be able to bring into perspective the fundamental institutions of society, showing how one interlocks with another in bringing about the highest happiness—the one goal of all human endeavor. To the extent that anything is explained, it is explained in its relation to other things. The danger to be guarded against in interpreting any movement is that of the "illusion of the near." A tourist may stand so close to the forest that he cannot see it for the trees; one may concentrate on a part of an intricate machine and never be able to comprehend the whole. In seeking, therefore, the politico-economic perspective, we would escape that narrow interpretation of events which is the result of a merely sectional or microscopic examination of them —an interpretation which may be false—in favor of that broader view which, taking into account as much of the situation as may be covered with the aid of our modern sociological telescope, will more completely envisage the social scene. In this way it will be seen that all the popular movements of to-day are part and parcel of the onward sweep of humanity, now so evident throughout the entire world.

In our perspective, the industrial, educational, religious and governmental institutions appear as being what they are—fundamental to any civilization. An examination of these institutions as they exist to-day will show, first of all, that they were built in an age different from ours; but, more particularly as far as our present purpose is concerned, it will show that they fail to respond in their present forms to the needs of modern society and are breaking down beneath the urgent demands of the new conditions.

People generally have been overawed by the seeming stability and unchangeability of things as they exist. Reared in certain settled opinions, there has been for them difficulty in realizing that the things which they have thought of as fixed at one time did not exist. The general public to-day might be represented as a man who has lived in his father's old home since birth. He has watched the rafters decay and time wear holes in the roof, but actuated by his reverence for the past has made no repairs, and at last unfavorable elements have demolished it.

So it has been with society. In the storm and stress of the collapsing social order, we are called upon to rebuild with such speed as to endanger the quality of the structure. Awakened suddenly from the ultra-conservatism which denies all change, we are faced with the startling realization that the only thing that never changes is the fact that all things change.

Institutions resemble living organisms; born and mothered in human need, they fight for existence against the forms which they are destined to supersede, then, passing through a period of adequate service, they decay and die. He is historically blind who would condemn all institutions at their source, as has been done, for instance, in the case of slavery, for it may be laid down as a truism that no institution can come into being and persist unless it is called for by some necessity. By this same law, institutions must cease to exist when they fail to perform the function for which nature designed them. Thus it happens that no truth can be permanently hindered, and no falsehood is endowed with eternal life.

Four years of war have tested the efficiency, as well as the morality, of our ways of doing things. We witness now in every department of human activity the struggle for readjustment. The cry of humanity has been raised above the cry of commercial greed. The cry of the soul goes out to the church for a deeper interpretation of life. The aspirations of intellect, broadened by the demands of modern life, are knocking at the doors of our educational institutions, and the voice of democracy thunders its challenge to the autocratic governments of civilization.

In the midst of the present unrest, largely caused by the growing pains of a new civilization, there are those who look upon the future with fear. They see their beloved past thrown into the melting pot of the present. Customs, creeds, and systems long revered, and around which are gathered affectionate sentiments, seem threatened with destruction from the crackling fire beneath the melting pot. But history, with a note of assurance, whispers to the faltering that there is nothing to fear; for eternal truth, refined as gold by the fire, will stand every test. Society is on the threshold of a new order. The old is passing away and all things are becoming new. It is not a time for fear, but a time for hope. Democracy turns her face toward the dawn and steps forward with courage into the new day.

THE FARMERS IN POLITICS

The herald of the new age comes in the form of a new social ethics. Everywhere there is evidence of a spirit entirely different from that which was the expression of the individualistic past. The time is hardly yet gone by when money-getting was the *sine qua non* of success. Many instances in the commercial history of Canada might be quoted in proof of a mercenary spirit which has possessed the nation to such an extent as to relegate the vital human interests to a secondary place. I shall have occasion later on to mention specific cases of business dealings which must be regarded, in the light of a new day, as soulless plunderings indicative of social blindness. The moral standards recognized between individuals in the affairs of common life, or as have been practised between neighbors, have many times and almost universally been disregarded in business and politics. Certainly legal punishments and social ostracism befell those who openly violated the golden rule in minor matters, but this notwithstanding it is even more certain that positions of honor and power were awarded to those who were successful in amassing wealth without question being raised as to the extent to which the golden rule was applied to larger transactions. No connection was seen to exist between the social outcast or vagrant and those who by virtue of their riches received popular acclaim. A better knowledge of economics, however, has since revealed the fact that in a socialized world there is the closest possible relation between the extensive private heritage of the few, and the disinheritance of the many. That extreme wealth finds its necessary counterpart in extreme poverty is now a matter of common knowledge. Following this knowledge is a sense of shame on the part of those who have been successful in a business world governed by the laws of the jungle.

That is why I say that the unscrupulous profiteer stands abashed before the searchings of Canada's new spirit. During recent years Canadian people have been forced to make a comparison between the volunteers for democracy and the profiteers of autocracy. In the light of the democratic ideal men fought and died in Flanders, while, at the very moment of the ordeal, there were those who did not hesitate to use the calamities of the nation as a means of gaining wealth. Canada has compared in her imagination the spirit of Flanders—the spirit of to-morrow—with the spirit of the profiteer—the spirit of yesterday; and has committed herself to the former. The socially atavistic are being weeded out; atavism is a continually rarer phenomenon. Yesterday is passed, to-morrow is not yet; this is the twilight of the gods.

The new spirit was no doubt generated in the midst of economic oppression. It is variously named; with religionists we may call it the coming of the Kingdom of God on earth; or in terms of the returned soldier, it may be called comradeship in national life; or again it may be seen as brotherhood extended to all practical affairs. Co-operation is but another aspect of the same thing. Nomenclature is of little significançe; the all-important thing is that a new spirit is present. It is reflected in the shame that is beginning to manifest itself among the rich; it is driving home the shaft of conviction to the plutocratic heart. True it is that income tax and public agitation against profiteering may to some extent account for the elaborate refutation of alleged dividends on the part of certain Canadian companies. A decade ago a headline in the daily press announcing that So-and-So had cleaned up a million would have been pleasant. So-and-So would have held his head a little higher that morning, and expanded his chest to the full. Not so to-day. When government commissions charge companies with profiteering, large amounts of space are purchased in the press to prove that it is not so. And why? Surely it is partly because the general public is aware of the means by which great wealth is made, either by individuals or by companies. It has discovered that no man, however brainy, that no company, however well-managed, can make millions unless permitted by a vicious privilege to reap where others have painfully sown; and Canada in her new spirit arises to brand this "thieving." Those who have used such privileges with impunity are scurrying for cover from the accusation and righteous indignation of an aroused public.

One of the great teachers of men virtually said: "If you have new wine and you want to save that new wine, you had better make new bottles to put it in; for if you pour your new wine into your old dried-skin bottles, they will break and you will lose your new wine." The application is obvious. The mission of the United Farmers and of all organized workers is simply to construct a repository for the new spirit of justice. To pour the new wine of co-operation into the old dried-skin bottles of cut-

25

throat competition, or, if you prefer, to pour the new wine of political democracy into the old bottles of party politics, is, in either case, to lose the new wine. To the agrarian worker in his environment of honest toil, and to the awakened worker of the industrial system in our cities, we look for the new measures and the new men which our times demand.

§2

Business and Service. Industry is the basis of national existence. The nature of man's struggle for the means of life is the foundation of the society in which he lives, and decides, in the main, its forms. Without accepting or rejecting the principle of economic determinism, it will be generally conceded that institutions in all ages have been fundamentally affected, if not conditioned, by the prevailing industrial system. This being so, evidence of change taking place in modern industrialism should be evidence of corresponding change taking place, or about to take place, in all other institutions.

Given incalculable natural resources, and a nation of willing workers, it follows as the night the day that there should be no poverty. If

poverty therefore exists under such conditions—
and no one will be found to deny that it does—
we must look elsewhere than to the causes generally given for the reason a problem of this
kind has to be faced.   Canada, with natural
resources beyond all computation, and with
thousands of willing workers ready to apply
their labor power to these resources for the production of wealth, is not exempt from poverty.
In this great land of the last chance, as well as in
European countries, from which people have
fled from the pains of poverty, the howls of the
wolf of hunger disturb the rest of many homes.
Already the slum, the crowning disgrace of civilization, has developed in our Canadian cities to
an extent not exceeded by anything to be found
in London or New York.   It is no uncommon
thing to see armies of unemployed parading our
streets in search of work, and as time passes,
strikes grow more frequent and more and more
portentous.

In reviewing the whole field of struggle, there
seems to be no possibility of evading the verdict
of the radical economists, that there is something
the matter with our industrial system.   But
what *is* wrong?   If natural resources are abundant, capable of yielding more than sufficient sup-

port for every national need, and if machinery has solved the problem of production, why poverty? Here we have the terms of the particular economic problem to be solved to-day. Doctors of economy have been diagnosing the disease of our industrial system for generations. As might be expected, there has not been entire agreement between those engaged in research as to what was the cause of the trouble; but one thing is certain, and that is that the economic thinking of recent years has amply demonstrated that the whole aim of modern production is wrong.

No one will deny that the aim of all industry and commerce to-day is profit. Human need underlies all industry; without human need it would be superfluous. If we needed nothing it goes without saying that we would not waste time satisfying a need that did not exist. But our industrial system takes this fundamental fact into account only to the extent that human need lends itself to exploitation. While all industry exists because of human needs, no industry is run solely for the purpose of supplying them. A secondary aim has usurped the place of the primary one, or has been superimposed on it by the course of the historical development of industry itself. The primary function of industry is lost sight of by promoters who take it as their prerogative to exploit the needs of man for profit-making for individuals. Thus our competitive system is one grand race for profit-making. There are no competitors for service. Service is incidental in the industrial scheme.

To this stupid state of affairs may be attributed the seething unrest which to-day is sweeping over civilization. The aim to make profit expresses itself in the whole industrial machine. It shows itself in long hours of labor and in small wages; and in unemployment, which is but another expression of the anarchy that underlies our system of production. Industrial promoters produce only that which is profitable. Even in the face of national peril, the manufacturer would rather produce hairpins than munitions, if there were more money to be made in hairpins. The profit-making aim, indeed, was so often demonstrated during the war that the individualistic principle in industry has been universally discredited.

The pressure of a crisis is the severest test of institutions as well as of individuals. The moment of crisis is like a searchlight on character; it reveals the coward or the hero with equal vividness. The great war subjected humanity to a most rigorous test, and humanity was not found wanting. Courage, that admirable human quality, was found to be universal. Established institutions, on the other hand, did not fare so well during this time of testing. The exigencies of the war inexorably revealed the weak spots of our institutional life, and the competitive system in all countries practically crumbled beneath the pressure of the national crisis. Unity of purpose for national service was the urgent need of the time, but the competitive system, which had bred the crisis, provided us with no means of securing this unity of purpose, as unity of purpose was the very antithesis of its competitive nature; it furnished us on the other hand with an industrial anarchy which, had it not been arrested in time, would have resulted in inevitable defeat. The common danger focussed all thought instantly on a national issue. So far this was a distinct gain, as at ordinary times, and in the absence of such danger, the social mind was too dissipated and spread over insistently egoistic pursuits, and purely individualistic ends. The need of war, however, which was an essentially national undertaking, created the necessity which led to our having to abandon the personal outlook for the communal. It was discovered that the *esprit de corps* of the national army must be transfused into the armies which were engaged in the basic industries of the country. But such a spirit could not enter a competitive system which permitted the few to profiteer at the expense of the exploitation of the many. The natural and logical step then was to proceed with the re-organization of industry on the basis of national service. To some extent this was done in all countries engaged in the great war.

Great Britain has furnished us with the outstanding example of the collapse of industrial individualism. The national leaders were confronted with the spectre of disaster. The British people were within sound of the bursting shells, and frequent visits from death-dealing aeroplanes left no room for illusion as to the nature of the conflict. For them it was a matter of national life. Every energy had to be centered on the common cause of national salvation. This common spirit stood out in relief against the profit-making of individual promoters. Although competition in industry, and the rights of private property, had long been looked upon as inviolate, these were shown, under pressure of the world struggle, to be at variance with the best interests of the people. National service was thrown into the scales of necessity against private interests, and thus weighed in the balance, full in view of an on-looking world, capitalism was found wanting.

Re-organization began forthwith; the British government immediately undertook to bring the basic industries of the country into line. Transportation, coal mines, and lands, hitherto looked upon as the private property of those who were in control, were taken over by the government and operated in the interests of the nation. In this way the waste through competition was eliminated; service was substituted for profit as the aim of the industries; and labor unrest, arising out of the consciousness that under private ownership national calamity was being exploited by profiteers, was effectively settled.

The words of Premier Lloyd George in his appeal to the people prior to effecting the changes above mentioned, were prophetic; and, judging from subsequent events, met with a more universal response than the Premier at that time anticipated. The theme of the Premier's message was that we had been launched into a new social order; and that we could never return to the old system we had left behind. He said to the British workmen in tones that rang around the world: "Men, be audacious in your demands, for we can never go back to the old ways again." Organized Labor in Great Britain took the Premier's words at their face value, and in the after-the-war period it is just a little more audacious in its demands than is comfortable for the Premier. For, almost unbelievable as it is, the Premier himself is among the first to attempt to go back. The whole struggle in Great Britain, since the cessation of hostilities, has been centered on the nationalization of basic industries. New political alignments have been made; Lloyd George and his Tory cabinet has combined with the landlords, mine-owners, and railroad magnates, to re-establish the old competitive system; while organized Labor and the common people generally have been, and still are, struggling to maintain national ownership.

The interest in Canada, of course, does not lie in the struggle now taking place in Great Britain; it rather lies in the fact that individualism in industry, after having been demonstrated to be inefficient, and after having been replaced by national ownership during the war, seems once more to be looming into view, and the question becomes one as to whether we are after all to revert to the old form of industry, or whether we are to retain the change already made, and hold fast to the adoption of the principle of national service in our national life.

Canada, removed from the actual scene of the conflict, was never fully alive to the meaning of the changes taking place in Europe. The pressure in Canada was too little felt. One of the proofs that the impact of the war on our populace was only slight, and our reaction to it superficial, is to be found in the fact that the Canadian commercial interests were never for a moment deflected from their "almighty dollar" philosophy. Their motto, adopted shortly after the outbreak of the war, was printed on posters and cards and distributed broadcast throughout the land. It read: "Business as Usual." Behind this motto there was doubtless a spirit of bravado; the profiteers wished all and sundry to think that wars might come and wars might go, but they went on (business as usual) forever. It may be that this motto was designed as an aid to *morale;* but it is quite likely that it was designed also as a blatant vindication of that very spirit and practice in industry from which Great Britain so early found it necessary to depart.

But since the printing of our "Business as Usual" posters, the Canadian people have had much cause to think, and have subjected the "Business as usual" principle to a close scrutiny and keen analysis. To the question, what does "Business as usual" mean, the answer comes that it means every man for himself and the devil take the hindmost—as usual; it means the erection of palatial residences in one section of the city, and the building of slums in another— slums in which the future citizens of Canada are living in ignorance, disease, and filth. "Business as usual" means that the price of wheat must be fixed when it starts to go up, (so that the farmer may not benefit by the *advance*) while the price of machinery necessary to farming is fixed only when it starts to go down, (again, so that the farmer may not benefit by the *decrease*). "Business as usual" will never be forgotten in Canada, for, while men were dying by the thousand, and our country was in anguish, the profiteers were amassing wealth. They also took a license wider than usual, wider that is than the ordinary "Business as usual" ethics permitted, and, as a result, the country was degraded by shell scandals, munition scandals, Ross rifle scandals, pork scandals, gravel and corruption scandals, and much of the time of the administration in power was occupied in considering these scandals and appointing fruitless Royal Commissions still further to consider them; and after they had been considered out of existence, the time of the administration in power was once more taken up in listening to the reports of commissions (costly as usual)—which reports ended in whitewashing the culprits, (as usual).

It will be seen then, that the industrial system in vogue in Canada has proved itself to be a failure both from the point of view of efficiency and from that of morality. Unlike Great Britain, Canada blundered through the crisis without effecting any material change in industrial methods; but the many lessons furnished by the war period have not been lost on the public mind; the new spirit indicated in an earlier section is beginning to be heard in the incessant and insistent demand for the humanizing of the industrial system. The new aim which some day will be crystallized in a new national policy for Canada will be to make happy human beings, instead of high profits.

Organized Labor is awake throughout the Dominion, and is seeking the subjection of profiteering aims to the aim of higher human values. It is also seeking to introduce the principle of democracy into industrial management, and demanding that labor, which is being sold to-day in the cheapest market, shall be redeemed from the status of a commodity. Labor is organizing against a system which metes out a bare existence to the thousands who produce the wealth, while the few who control the means of wealth production roll in the fatness of the land. It stands opposed to a system which produces jobless men, and in favor of the inauguration of a new order in which all may have work, and in which all will be able to reap the benefits of their toil. The problem which industry at the present day presents, is no longer a bone of contention merely between Capital and Labor; it is one of national and human importance. It is becoming more imperative that the nation must undertake to find work for its citizens, or to feed those for whom it cannot find work. A matter which involves the very life of the people can no longer be left to the caprice of individuals in search of profit. The movement, everywhere, is towards the nationalization of basic industries, aiming at democratic control and the principle of service. These important matters are gradually being solved even while we write about them. There is not likely to be anything of a cataclysmic nature in passing from individualism into the commonwealth, and from competition to co-operation. The main thing is to be reconciled to the idea that the old system is not going to be re-built, and that we proceed to lay the new foundation for society, as the needs of the hour determine.

§3

Education and Life. Industry touches life at the very center. Any drastic economic change will speedily reflect itself in society as a whole. It is therefore in keeping with natural progress to discover even with regard to our educational institutions an urgent desire for a readjustment to modern demands, which will correspond in its nature and spirit to the admitted agitation in the industrial world. Like the life blood in the veins which courses through the whole organism, democracy, if adopted must permeate the whole system of society. It cannot be shut off at the ballot box, or limited to a recognized right of the people to organize. If we commit ourselves to the democratic principle, there must be no isolating it, no restricting it within certain bounds, no field in which it will be a trespasser; it must spread everywhere. Education in a democracy is of supreme importance. At this stage democracy is more a problem than a solution. It remains to be worked out. The great benefits which democracy is destined to bestow will naturally be equalled by the responsibilities it will bring. Responsibility must be removed from the shoulders of a few to the shoulders of all, and this implies a universal fitness for responsibility which education alone can give. In other words, if we are going to have a democratic state, we must democratize education, and bring our educational institutions into line with democratic ideals.

Education is not to-day, either in aim or in equality of opportunity, democratic. The aim, in so far as there is an aim in modern education, is to maintain the *status quo,* its autocracy and injustice notwithstanding, while the inequality of opportunity in respect of obtaining an education is too glaring for comment. A writer in a leading current educational journal expresses the situation in rather strong language: "The spiritual bankruptcy of our school system is the appalling, the deeply disheartening fact of our day and generation; the great war has revealed our educational system as a vast Prussianized enterprise, quantitatively impressive, qualitatively moribund." A study of the whole system would give justification for this view. That people are becoming aware of the state of affairs is evident from the incidents which will be dealt with directly.

The backward state of education is amply demonstrated by the status ascribed to the teaching profession. The salaries paid to teachers, and especially to teachers in rural schools, are not only deplorable, but disgraceful. Measuring the teachers' salaries by the cost of living, it will be found that the remuneration for doing what should be the most exalted service, is entirely inadequate, taking into account what it costs to live. When comparing the salaries of teachers with the remuneration for service in other fields, the result is such as to render the teaching profession very unattractive. Men have, in consequence, been driven from the profession, and driven solely by economic necessity. Women without family responsibilities have replaced the men. In every state in the United States, and in most provinces in Canada, there is an alarming shortage of qualified teachers.

THE PROCESS OF READJUSTMENT

Thousands of schools are in the care of poorly prepared girls scarcely out of their teens, and even so, there is still a shortage; and what is worse, the shortage notwithstanding, the salaries paid are so low that for very self preservation the teachers are being forced to combine in unions of one sort and another throughout the whole American continent. Canada has already witnessed the disgrace of a teachers' strike. The disgrace, of course, does not reflect on the teachers, but on the governments and people who have so blindly neglected to attend properly to the most important institution in modern society.

But what is the background of this picture? Why are not teachers paid as high a wage as the flunkies of the rich, and why the apathy on the part of the general public, which has permitted this state of affairs to develop? The answer, in part at least, seems to be that institutionalized education has little to do with common life, and offers only small help in the solution of the problems that are pressing hardest on the public mind.

The masses of the people have not been much interested in schools in the past because their children got next to nothing from them, many children of the working class not even being able to attend the public school for a length of time sufficient to obtain the rudiments of that which is commonly called education. True, there are compulsory laws for the benefit of the recalcitrant, but there are laws more effective than statute laws, and these will not be gainsaid. Rent and food speak louder than the statutes and they call the children of the workers to the factory and to the plough long before education is well commenced.

High Schools and Universities exist for the wealthy. These places of learning, although financed by taxes imposed on the poor, are but additional privileges for the rich. Few boys and girls from the farms pass through high school, while it would appear that the percentage of the city children of the working class who receive secondary education is even smaller than that of rural districts. It is not, therefore, to be wondered at that there is a growing agitation in the ranks of organized farmers and in labor unions for radical changes along educational lines. This popular demand, voiced so often by workers in convention, is being supported by teachers' unions, and leading educationalists are beginning to stir. The educational conference held at Winnipeg in October, 1919, although fruitless in many important respects, showed that even in the ranks of the cultured the need for drastic educational reconstruction is being recognized.

Vocational training has been sadly neglected. The stamp of our commercial age is placed on every curriculum. The great important industries of life have counted, up till now, for only little in our elementary schools. The saying that children have been educated away from the farm has a deal of truth in it. It is not suggested here that education should be entirely vocational in character. Were that the case, our condition might be even worse. But it does seem that when a young man or woman leaves school, he or she should be qualified to do some useful work, and further that no education can rightfully be considered adequate that neglects to prepare its pupils for their after life. A rural school, for instance, that does not have in its curriculum subjects relating to agriculture, would be as much out of place as an Atlantic liner on the prairie. Education to be complete must make connection with life at every point.

That the drift is in the direction of an education for life there is ample proof. Physical culture, vocational training, hygiene, and the laws of health, as well as moral culture and citizenship, are commanding greater attention, and are being pushed forward as more essential to the life of society than classics, or higher mathematics. The Federal department recently created in the United States, involving an expenditure of $100,000,000 annually, is one indication that a response is coming to the fundamental calls of life. The Federal act by which this new department was created embodies such things as the removal of illiteracy, the Americanization of foreigners, equalization of opportunity, education in health, physical culture and recreation, etc. The Education Acts of England and Scotland passed in 1918 are also encouraging, while signs are not lacking that Canada, also, is awakening to a true appreciation of what education should mean to the nation.

The widespread agitation for greater educational facilities and for a broader and deeper interpretation of the aim of education itself, which has been prevalent in Great Britain and America for years, and which has been partly met by the Educational Acts recently put upon the statute books of these countries, has sprung from a deep-rooted urgency in a society that is being rapidly transformed. The underlying motive impelling men and women to seek for themselves and their children a better education is the desire to obtain a fuller self-expression; the urge within making always toward a more adequate development of personality. A fuller life is demanded not only in the gaining of a greater measure of the necessaries of life, but in the developing the capacity for the enjoyment of life implied in moral, intellectual, and aesthetic culture.

The social purpose underlying the educational movement of our time is of quite as much significance as the desire for a fuller personal life. That citizenship in a democracy is being appreciated is shown by the willingness with which social responsibility is being accepted. Democracy might be defined as the socialization of responsibility. Hitherto individuals have thought and acted for the mass. Such an arrangement was more secure while the masses were in ignorance, and the individuals had a monopoly of knowledge, but the security and well-being of society to-day depend upon the fitness of the masses to bear the responsibilities of citizenship. Aware of this greater responsibility, the people are seeking to prepare themselves for it. Continuation classes, the raising of the age limit to which children may be compelled to attend school, the phenomenal spread of the idea of public forums for the discussion of public questions, all point toward an increased interest, which is healthy and prophetic of an educated public.

Another renaissance is approaching. It will not consist in the wholesale importation of the culture of an ancient people, as was done in the fifteenth century. There is no such an advanced people to-day standing in relation to the present civilized world as Greece and Rome stood to Europe at the time of the renaissance. Our task is therefore to create, not to copy. Transportation and communication in their modern efficiency have brought the nations of the earth together, with the result that what is known to one may be known by all. The New Learning of our age is going to result from the demands which our own lives make upon us. Its chief characteristics will consist in its being linked more closely to life, and in obtaining a more definite and more serviceable aim.

It is perhaps advisable to say something here about what is meant by bringing education into harmony with life, and to state how the aims of education are being interpreted by those who are in the struggle for educational improvement. The end of civilization as set forth in the reconstruction of the British Labor Party may be quoted with profit as summing up the object that will constitute the goal of the coming era. "If we in Britain are to escape from the decay of civilization itself . . . we must assume that what is presently to be built up is a new social order, based not on fighting but on fraternity; not on the competitive struggle for the means of bare life, but a deliberately planned co-operation in production and distribution for the benefit of all who participate by hand or brain; not on the utmost inequality of riches, but on a systematic approach towards a healthy equality of material circumstances for every person born into the world; not on an enforced dominion over subject nations, subject races, subject colonies, subject classes, or a subject sex, but, in industry as well as in government, on that equal freedom, that general consciousness of consent, and that widest possible participation in power, both economic and political, which is characteristic of democracy." Here is a new Magna Charta of civilization. The problems involved in this outlook are on the social conscience. Education will not be education if it does not prepare the coming generations for the enormous task so nobly and courageously set forth.

It may be doubted if the civilization that is just passing away had any conscious aim. More truly may it be said that the industrial era has been guided by the primitive instinct which resulted, in the economic as well as in the biological field, in the "survival of the fittest." Nothing was planned deliberately. No human being ever planned a slum, or deliberately divided society into "the shearers and the shorn"; poverty did not come at the behest of any individual, class, or government; monopoly, of which poverty is the corollary, was not consciously engaged in. Like Topsy, it grew. Ours has been a planless civilization. Anarchy in industry, and "catch as catch can" in distribution were the characteristics of capitalism. How, then, could there be an aim in education, when there was anarchy everywhere else? All that could be done was to prepare one for efficiency in the scramble.

The great thought of Ruskin, "that there is no wealth but life; that that country is the richest which nourishes the greatest number of noble and happy human beings," is coming into vogue, and will constitute the immediate end of education in the future. To prepare people to make a living in a way that will justify their right to live, and to prepare people to enjoy life in such a way as to make it worth while living, might be said to be in a general sense the new ideal sought after. In following this ideal education will fulfil its true function, and so most adequately contribute to the happy future of society.

I may have been too sanguine in my reflections here, and there may be those who will hasten to compare education as it is with the aims and standards hinted at in this chapter. Should this be done, it will undoubtedly be found that our existing educational institutions are far behind in the comparison. Even so, I am dealing with the tendency. Everything cannot be accomplished in a day. The call comes to our schools and universities as it comes to every department of our complex life; all alike are challenged by an ever-changing society. Response is being made and must continue to be made, until education leads out into the world of human happiness, and until every child in the state shall have an equal opportunity to follow where it leads.

4

§4

The Modern Religious Appeal. No true perspective of society as it exists to-day is possible if religion is excluded. The religion here referred to is that which is inseparable from the interpretation which people give to life, not the narrow concept which, centering around creeds and churches, often passes for religion. We are constantly advised by politicians to keep religion out of politics. There has been too much of this advice given; and it must be said with regret that if religion stands for anything of moral value those who advocate keeping it out of politics are entirely successful. There is a kind of religion, however, which some politicians would fare badly without. It is a well-known fact that frequently during elections certain differences of religious opinion are used by unscrupulous politicians as a means of pitting one section of the community against another. What would certain politicians do if they could not play Quebec against Ontario by means of the religious differences between the inhabitants of these provinces? It is deplorable that this continues to be done at the present day; and more especially that it is only by a most generous interpretation that these differences of opinion can be held even remotely to touch on religion at all. Religion in political campaigning is the filthy rags of creedal bias, used for the purpose of obscuring the issue proper. Such a degradation of religion is to be deplored and condemned.

My purpose in referring to religion does not involve a discussion of the relative merits of creeds, sects, or churches, nor does it admit any consideration of the question in its theological aspect. I am concerned only with the new social appeal which indicates a reinterpretation of that deeper spiritual truth for which religion stands. The trend of religious thought, as expressed by church conferences and from the pulpits, is away from the old individualistic outlook, and more and more towards making a social application of Christian principles. It can scarcely be doubted that the individualism which prevailed in industry reflected itself in religion as preached during the industrial period. This, coupled with an otherworldism which tended to neglect the pressing problems of the present life, has greatly hampered the influence of the church in recent generations. But religion to-day has a wider appeal. The individual appeal may still find its place, and otherworldism may still have a part in the church's program; but there is also the recognition that whatever world there may be beyond this, character will be determined there largely by what we are here, and also that environment here, including social conditions here, and how we make our living here, are vital factors in making that character. In other words, it is now recognized to be impossible to save the world one individual at a time as long as the conditions from which people need to be saved are allowed to go unchallenged.

The task of the church to-day is to save the soul of society, and there are indications that the church will meet that task in the true spirit of her founder. The great *public* vices are being attacked with that determination and enthusiasm which characterized the religious efforts against *personal* vice in years gone by. The Drink Traffic, Graft, Profiteering, Greed, Monopoly, Competition, Individualism, and Poverty, are being arraigned from every quarter as incompatible with Christian principles. In a very real sense the protests against these public iniquities have been inspired by true religion. The protest may come from a Labor Hall, a church conference, a U.F. convention—but whatever its place of origin the spirit is the same. It denounces a system of society that makes paupers by the million and millionaires by the score; a society which compels the many to struggle for a bare existence while utterly denied opportunities of soul development, and driven and harried from day to day by the grim fear of want. The new religious spirit is the very soul of the world movement for justice. It is the champion of the weak against the strong; it elevates the human values to a height of paramount importance in the whole system of human affairs; and stands for conditions of life which are conducive to the highest morality both in individual character and national life.

This kind of religion cannot be kept out of politics. Being inseparable from life it permeates its every department, and extends the domain of the sacred to what have been called material things. The line between the sacred and secular is being rubbed out. This does not mean that everything is becoming secular; on the contrary, everything is becoming sacred. In the past the sacred things of life have been extremely limited. We had but one sacred day in seven, one sacred building in a community, one sacred calling in all the vocations of men, and one sacred book in all literature. The decided tendency on the part of the church to extend the limits of the sacred is perhaps the surest indication of the reinterpretation of Christianity that is coming in response to the need of our times. The day is coming when the land by which we live will be considered as sacred as the little plot in which we bury our beloved dead. When that time fully arrives there will be no more speculation in land, for the privileged few who now hold out of use land which should be utilized in growing bread will no longer be able to do so. When that time comes, the privileged few will have disappeared. We are approaching the time when every employment will have service for its aim, and will be looked upon as being as sacred as that of a clergyman. And just think what a day it will be when our factories become sacred—so sacred that there will be no sweating, no exploitation, no unsanitary conditions—and when the man who would not perform a bad deed on Sunday will find that all other days have also become sacred. It is not difficult to worship God in church for an hour on Sunday. There we find beauty, music, and an atmosphere that is spiritually uplifting. But it is not so easy to worship God in the factory, or on the lonely homestead. The church is going to help to bring about conditions under which men and women will be able to live in an attitude of worship; that is, they will find a joy in work of service, and a self-expression which will be truly religious, and the hunger, and hatred, and strife, which are inevitable under prevailing conditions, will be swept away.

To make all life sacred is in a general sense the goal toward which religious activity is tending. The church has not been wholly deaf to the challenge of the times, and although slow to move she has not altogether ignored it. There is a new note sounding from the pulpits, and a new outlook that not only bespeak the changing times in which we live, but point to the better day toward which we are travelling.

§5

Moral Degeneration of the Party System. Governmental forms are no more permanent than industrial or educational forms. Governments take their forms from the economic basis upon which they rest, and for which they function. The divine right of kings fitted well with the feudalism of the middle ages; and the plutocratic oligarchies of the United States and Canada are the natural outgrowth of an era based on industrial individualism; and as these earlier forms of the state have been the reflex of the societies of the time, so also must the governments of to-morrow be reshaped to correspond to the industrial democracy which is now in process of being established.

For several generations the two-party system of government, which has been carried to its logical conclusion in the histories of Great Britain and Canada, has been developing serious weaknesses, and is gradually losing its fitness to function as the expression of the economic forces struggling for supremacy to-day. Whenever a thing continues to exist after the need for it has disappeared, its funeral is overdue. No matter how serviceable the party system may have been at one time, (and in justice to truth its serviceableness cannot be disputed) it has fallen away from the original purpose for which it was intended. Its chief aim to-day is to maintain its own existence.

To recount: The ancient principle which justified the birth of the parties gradually weakened and gave place to partyism which ultimately became a sort of fetish to which people blindly and rigidly adhered. When principle was lost, partyism had to resort to other means of sustaining itself. When there was no real national issue, false issues had to be created merely for election purposes; corruption crept in to an alarming degree; graft and patronage eventually were considered as a matter of course, indispensable to the party system; political campaigns grew more expensive, and in consequence the parties became the tools of the wealthy. In fact it may be said that partyism became an investment for big interests in Canada, dividends being paid in the shape of legislation and privileges to those in a position financially and morally to make the investment. Business interests no longer content themselves with financing one of the parties—they donate freely to the campaign funds of both, and so make doubly sure of purchasing government influence, no matter which party happens to be elected. Thus our government machinery has grown to be the most farcical of institutions, being used by the wealthy as a means of attaining financial advancement, and applied to the masses for the purpose of dividing them foolishly against themselves, dividing them in fact to such an extent as to render them politically helpless.

Between the parties, any difference of an economic nature has long since ceased to exist. In organization, in lack of principle, and in practical misgovernment, the Tory and Liberal parties are identical. The unbiased will be left quite unable to decide in favor of tweedledum or tweedledee, even after the closest investigation. It would be an extremely interesting thing to test party supporters on the difference they claim to see between their respective parties. Take, for instance, the statute books of Canada since Confederation, erase the dates from various measures, and then submit them to party men for a decision as to which party was in power when they were passed. It is a safe wager that no one who was not thoroughly acquainted with Canadian history would be able to tell. It will be found that Liberal administrations have sustained the tariff, while, in some instances, Conservative governments have lowered it. Sir Wilfrid Laurier practically sustained the tariffs of Sir John A. Macdonald. In 1894, the duty on agricultural implements was 20 per cent. This duty was practically the same at the close of the Laurier regime. Again, in 1906 there was a reduction of 2½ per cent. on some farm implements, but this was immediately followed by an increase in appraised value which in reality increased the price of farm machinery. The Liberals were adepts at reducing tariffs on the hustings, but they failed signally to do it to any great extent in parliament. On the other hand, the Conservatives have been known to reduce tariffs, and even in Parliament, where one would have expected them to be immovable. In 1885 coke was put on the free list; and in 1887 the duty was repealed on anthracite coal by a Conservative government. Then Sir Robert Borden's government put wheat on the free list and made a reduction of the tariff on farm machinery. It cannot be said, therefore, that the tariff is the point of difference between the Liberal and the Conservative. History shows us otherwise. In any case, those who benefit by tariff have sufficient influence with either party to obtain exactly what they want. Both parties exist to serve privilege, and all their time is taken up doing that. There is no more hope, for the people, in the one than in the other.

Party enthusiasts, confronted with such a test, will repair to the field of psychology for defence, and cite innumerable cases to prove that people are naturally either conservative or progressive, and that there is on account of this, a basis in nature for the existence of just such parties. People of opposed temperaments will inevitably express themselves through parties similarly opposed. There is no doubt of the truth of this contention. Both types are indispensable to progress. The part of the conservative is to hold, or conserve, the progress already made, while the progressive is chiefly interested in making more progress. The two are inseparable. Without the conservative element, we would not only be in danger of going back, but we would never develop sufficiently by practice to be prepared for the next step; while without the progressives, society would become static and decadent.

The fallacy of this argument is in using it as a justification for the party system. As a matter of fact, both these attitudes may be adopted by the same individual, in relation to the same problem—but in different circumstances. A person may be a conservative on one issue, and a radical on another. Partyism denies this natural liberty, and says if one is conservative on one policy one must commit oneself to the conservative side of all policies. Hence, partyism tends to reduce every person to uniformity of thought and action, and uniformity means death. Any organization which tends to limit expression to one sort of policy or another is in a fair way to bring about that static condition which the conservative and progressive types of mind seem to exist to prevent.

Just here there is a possibility that in attributing any such thought to partyism as is involved in the psychological argument, we are giving more credit to machine politics than is its due. In reality people who call themselves Liberal and Conservative, when required to give a reason for the faith that is in them, are dumb. But when a man of one party can give no sufficient reason why he does not belong to the other party, and yet fights that other party with an intense feeling amounting almost to hatred, it is high time to make enquiry into the so-called "glorious traditions" of the parties. Surely the time has come for people to give a better reason than that of tradition for the use they make of their franchise. It often happens that a man calling himself a Liberal cannot tell why he is not a Conservative, or *vice versa*. When this occurs there is something the matter either with his head or with his politics. As there are many such men, the charitable thing is to blame politics.

61

Between the parties in Canada there is no difference, as far as political economy is concerned; the difference is among the people, who, being born in Conservative or Liberal homes, have been nurtured in a particular party bias, and, in consequence, perform that duty of citizenship—the exercise of the franchise—through ancestral habit, instead of at the dictation of heart and mind, and instead of considering only the immediate issue and its ultimate effects. When the ancestral influence begins to wane, racial and religious differences are introduced as a means of destroying the effect of any economic opinion which might lead to concerted action on the part of those on whom the old influences no longer have any hold. The real election issues in Canada are created, as well as kept alive, by the wealthy. Only the wealthy can sustain an imaginary issue, because it requires millions systematically to misrepresent a question to the extent that people, on the strength of the misrepresentation, will vote against their own interests. To accomplish this, the press must be "got," literature must be prepared, published, and circulated, and posters of various kinds as well as cartoons must be provided. It was alleged, for example, that the Union Government party spent an unheard-of amount in propaganda and publicity prior to the election of 1917. If this, indeed, were the case, it was done owing to the fact that the Union party was preaching the gospel of the wealthy, by whom it was financed. That section of the Liberal party which did not follow the new political alignment had, it was said, little or no money to spend; neither had the labor party; and the farmers—well, the farmers were embarrassed no less by being in the same position. The result was that the public was educated almost without hindrance by financial interests to the acceptation of a totally false issue. Organizations were drawn away from their common interests by the emotional and even hysterical appeals of party press and demagogues. Neither in the election appeals of 1917 nor 1911 had national issues anything whatever to do. The 1911 election was won because the financial interests were able to make annexation to the United States the burning question, and in 1917 the electors were not permitted to see anything but the flag. Profiteering, the high cost of living, efficiency in production and distribution, and many other questions of public concern were obscured by the unceasing waving of the Union Jack, and of course people voted for the Union Jack. But the Union Jack never was an issue in Canada. It was used merely as a covering for political designs. That portion of the populace which saw through the political trickery was called disloyal, unpatriotic, pro-German, and alien enemies. And those who were carried to power on the crest of this patriotic sentiment have been well described by Dr. Johnson when he says of patriotism that it is "the last refuge of scoundrels."

Party finance has proved to be one of the most important factors leading to the moral degeneration of the party system. It has long been considered a truism that those who financed the parties ruled the country. Unfortunately the masses of the people have not yet been sufficiently interested in their own business to undertake the financing of their political affairs themselves directly. Those, however, who have been financing the political parties in the past have collected the necessary funds from the people, indirectly, in the form of high prices, taxes, and so on; and as well, by money compulsorily spent in Canada because high tariffs prevented from being imported, articles required for Canadian consumption. Part of this money eventually filtered into the party coffers. In some cases, too, even Government contracts have been used as a means of replenishing the exchequer. This scheme was worked by letting the contract to a privileged individual or company, which individual or company in return made a substantial donation to the party fund. If such contract was given at a reasonable figure, the contractor would have to turn out shoddy work in order to make up the amount to be donated. A case in point is the infamous Kelly contract in connection with the Parliament Buildings of Manitoba. This incident occurred during the Roblin regime, and is so well-known as hardly to require more than bare mention. The case became historic because the principals in the transaction were caught redhanded, but, just the same, party funds were secured, both before and after that event, and by similar means, without the public knowing anything about it.

Finance is the oil of the party machine, without which it would not be able to run. Consequently, the financial question determines many important things. It has much to do with the selection of a candidate. The wealthy man, provided he is a safe party man, invariably gets the preference. By a great many people it is considered, and indeed frequently said, that the election of good men, men that is with intellectual ability and moral principle, would be the solution of our political difficulties. If this be so, then under the party system there is no hope that they will ever be elected. Money is of more value, politically, than character. The result is that we have politicians in charge of our national and provincial affairs instead of statesmen. As an instance of the influence of money in the selection of representatives, I would mention a party convention, held in Northern Ontario, at which there was selected a candidate for the 1917 election. The spokesman of the convention, the editor of the party paper, in speaking against a farmers' candidate who had been nominated over the head of the machine, said: "We appreciate the interest which you men have taken in our party as shown in the nomination of Mr. ——————— as our standard-bearer. No doubt he is a good man, but that is not the only consideration. You know that elections are not won by prayer; most of you look like five dollars on election day whether you get it or not. This constituency has been spoiled by the rich man who has represented us for so many years, and who bought his way to power. The people expect to be bought. Anyway, it costs money to run an election. We have a candidate here who is fully qualified. You don't know him, and probably have never heard of him, but we can assure you that he has the money, and that means he will be elected. We cannot afford to risk our success upon a candidate who has no money." It goes without saying that the man with the money was chosen. While the foregoing speech may be more blunt and crude than usual, it accurately sets forth the essential characteristic of a party candidate. He must have money. A candidate might have the profoundest wisdom of the ancient sages, the moral and spiritual qualities of a Marcus Antoninus or a Christ, together with the persuasiveness of a Demosthenes, but without the money he would not qualify. In these circumstances, is it any wonder that Canada has so few statesmen in public life?

Next to having money, a candidate may be selected for his chameleon-like qualities which enable him to appear in the exact color of party thought; or again a man is sometimes chosen because he typifies the pretended cause as did certain returned officers in the war-times election.

But seldom if ever is a man selected because of his knowledge of political economy.

Since money chooses and elects candidates, it controls their actions when in parliament. There are only four ways of financing a party candidate. The first is, that the candidate pay his or her own expenses. This means, in most cases, that the first opportunity which will bring back the capital (and interest on the capital) invested in the election, will be embraced. Canada has few, if any, philanthropic politicians. If five or ten thousand dollars be spent, it will be required back—as soon as possible—and required with interest. This is natural, and politicians, for this, are not to blame. A people that tolerates such a system is placing a stumbling block before the honesty of its representatives. It is exactly that; what religious people term a "scandal"—a stumbling block; and until this condition of things is changed, the chance of improvement is practically nil.

The second way to finance an election is for the party to do it. In this case the representative becomes the party tool, and responds to every crack of the party whip. The third way is for some financial interest to pay the election expenses. When this happens it is done as an investment, which pays dividends in terms of legislation. The fourth way is for the people to go into their own pockets, and finance their own affairs, and thus assume responsibility and control. The movement is obviously in this direction to-day. The United Farmers took the initiative, and others are following.

§6

Party political platforms are another example of immoral practice. They are immoral, first, because they are hypocritical, promising something they never intend to perform; and next because they are used as baits for votes, which votes place all power in the hands of the enemies of the people. Platforms are made to get "in" on; they are the products of political exigency, and therefore are designed to be attractive from the point of view of the number of votes they may capture. Platforms, in one sense, are like sugar-coated pills; the patient who takes them is saved from the bitterness of the ingredients as long as the sugar coating lasts. In another sense, platforms are like baby soothers, invented to make the child believe it is obtaining food, while in reality it is receiving nothing but wind. The

Hypo-crisy.

effect of party platforms is precisely similar. Temporarily, they soothe the restive and put them to sleep; but sooner or later comes the cruel awakening, and realities of hunger, cold, and sore distress make themselves felt more intensely still. The people have been hoodwinked in this way so often that their confidence is at last at an end. The tendency to-day is to apply to every politician the statement of the ancient writer, "All men are liars." To undermine the confidence of man in his fellows is to lay the basis of anarchy, and yet, oblivious of the certain outcome, politicians have almost invariably broken their promises to the people, by consistently ignoring the platforms upon which they were elected. The systematic deception of politicians has done more to develop the revolutionary spirit that politicians fear, than all the speeches and propaganda of the so-called Bolsheviki.

In 1911 we were told that if farmers shipped wheat into the United States free of duty, or imported machinery free of customs tariff, Canada would thereby be annexed to the United States, and that a vote for reciprocity meant the "pulling down of the British flag which floated so proudly over the glory of the British Empire and all the heritages so dearly purchased by the blood of our forefathers." It was the unthinking margin that can always be swung by the emotional appeals of the demagogue that, together with the immovable party adherents, tendered Sir Robert Borden his majority as the "savior of our mighty empire." Sir Robert went to Ottawa, bowed his acknowledgment of the confidence of the Canadian people, and at once proceeded to do the very things which he had been elected not to do. He gave the farmers free wheat, and lowered the duty on machinery as proposed by the reciprocity pact. Sir Robert and his party claimed, during the campaign that Reciprocity (which did not imply anything more than a mutual arrangement of tariffs between Canada and the U.S.A.) was anti-British. But the Borden government did not hesitate to enact laws that implied the very principle which the government had been elected for condemning. Nevertheless, our empire is still intact, while the chicanery practised in this instance served but to further undermine the existing political system.

Although methods such as these are to be deplored, they still possess an educational value, in a negative sense at least, because they lead the people to a knowledge of what they do not want, even if they are hazy on what they do want. Partyism with its greed and servility, its disregard for truth, its graft, patronage, and corruption, is becoming nauseous, and parties are being compelled, by the sheer weight of public opinion, to give up their old names, and to adopt new methods. The question now is, will the people themselves find a substitute for the old parties and old methods, or will they allow themselves to be gulled once more by merely exterior changes adopted by the party leaders in distress? This question still awaits an answer.

Perhaps the moral and spiritual bankruptcy of our public life have led, more directly than any criticism, to the downfall of partyism. The party ambition to "win" regardless of the "how" of winning, has overshot its mark. Yet again, the election of 1917 provides us with an example of that ambition to win by fair means or foul, which has done so much to debase politics. The promise of the Union party to the farmers will not soon be forgotten. Spokesmen of the Union Government came to the farmers of Canada with an appeal something like the following: "Farmers, you are the backbone of this country. We come to you in this, the greatest crisis of our

national life. We come because you are a democratic people, and we are the government of a
democracy. We wish you to understand the
nature of the calamity with which we are confronted. You are aware that we are at war, that
we are at war to protect ourselves against the
rule of the Kaiser. Already the despicable
Huns are knocking at the golden gates of this
great Western Eldorado; our voluntary system
of raising an army has reached its limits, our
army is being depleted at a greater rate than it
is being recruited; if we cannot remedy this
state of things, the war is lost, and Canada will
fall into the hands of Germany. In this great
national crisis we seek from you a mandate for
the enforcement of conscription of men; but
before you vote, Mr. Farmer, we wish you to
understand that it is not your son that we want
to conscript. Ah, no! That would be disastrous.
We must keep up production. We want to see
your son behind the plough, raising wheat for
our armies; the men we wish you to help us
conscript are the hoboes and bohunks who frequent the pool-rooms of our towns and cities, the
slackers, in fact, who are shirking their duty to
the country, no matter where they are, nor who
they are, but not the tillers of the soil, nor those

without whose continued self-sacrificing service the country would be unable to carry on. Return us to Parliament, Mr. Farmer, and you may rest assured that you and your kind will not be touched by the measures we propose to put on the statute books for the conscription of non-producers and idlers." But scarcely was the Union Government settled at Ottawa when the message flashed across the Dominion that the sons of farmers never were meant to be exempted. Now, there is no objection to the universal application of conscription of men. If any are to be conscripted, all should be conscripted. In this the government was right. But what is to be thought of the morality of a party which, in order to get votes, virtually said to one man, "If you will vote to send that other man's son, where you don't want *your* son to go, we will exempt your son? This was said not only by the old Tory party but by Grits and Tories alike, who combined to form the party which became the Union Government. The leaders of both the old parties (with the honorable exception of Sir Wilfrid Laurier) lent themselves to an election war cry which they never at any time intended to enforce. It was a dishonest slogan from the start. Such is partyism in Canada. No public body, party, or organization, which made such an appeal, is morally fit to survive. Nor will it survive. It is dying from inward mortification. When the time comes for its interment, we will be the first to write, *Requiescat in pace*.

Incidentally, those who respond to the undemocratic appeal of party strategists are as culpable as the politicians who make the appeal. The value of any political promise consists in its attractiveness. An electorate which was not to be moved by an unfair promise, would never have an unfair promise given. The farmers of Canada who were caught in the political traps of 1911 and 1917 must confess to a hankering after the bait used in those traps. The Canadian public is responsible for the politicians. The public has made them what they are. But the appearance in our parliaments, recently, of a different type of men is the best proof, if proof were required, that the public mind is undergoing at last, and rapidly, a healthy change.

§7

Party System Obsolete

The moral degeneracy of party politics is not so much a cause as it is the effect of the downfall of the two-party system. The graft, the patronage, and the chicanery, resemble the putrid odor of the decaying carcass. The two party system is all but dead, having been brought into an economic environment in which life for it was impossible. The hypodermic injections so industriously administered by political leaders will not serve to resuscitate it. To shoot an electric current through a dead frog and make its legs move, creating a semblance of life, may be possible, but the frog does not live again; and the formation of new parties is analogous to electrifying the legs of a dead frog. New parties are not the remedy; for death there is no remedy. The glamor thrown over the system by the introduction of a new party acts like electricity on the frog; the party moves its legs, and even goes to Ottawa, but the system is paralysed and thoroughly decrepit. The two party system will never be revived, but an examination into the causes of its death—a post mortem—may be of service if it enable us quickly to be rid of a corpse, and also, if it aid us to discover the proper conditions of health for future political organizations.

Death, whether of an organism or of a political system, immediately ensues when there is a failure on the part of the internal to correspond with external changes. The longevity of the party system of government depends upon its ability to conform to the numerous changes inseparable from a highly organized and infinitely complex industrial civilization. The two party system was the child of the social plasm. It provided for one simple division of the cell, but stopped at that, remained simple, and ignored the drastic changes which the application of machinery in industry produced. In the comparatively simple organization of society which existed at the time when the two party system was introduced, it was possible to divide the people on the Yea or Nay side of most questions. There were no large industrial centers with their highly specialized groups. Most work was performed by handcraft, and the simplest form of commercialism prevailed. The industrial classes were in embryo, and still had common interests and understood each other. But with the social stratification brought about in the process of industrial evolution, the point has been reached when the industrial classes know less of each other's requirements than they did in the less complicated society. The pre-Copernican philosophy of our party system is absurd considering the complexity of modern life. I call the philosophy of partyism pre-Copernican because it assumes that every question is flat and has two ends, similar to the pre-Copernican idea of the physical world. This means that one must freeze into an icicle at the North Pole with the Tories or be passed off in vapor through equatorial heat with the Grits. But, just as the habitable world exists between these extremes, so also truth may be the mean between the poles of human thought. Every issue to-day is round like the world, and may be approached from any degree in the circumference of the circle. A legislative measure which had been voted upon Yea or Nay by the parties, would, if subjected to criticism from all quarters, be so modified as to be neither that which was accepted nor that which was rejected by the snap verdict, but would reflect the expert opinion of organized groups everywhere throughout the nation. In other words, there is no provision made in the party system for the expression of the varied interests developed of necessity by industrial organization. Our highly organized world refuses to divide itself into two halves, as did the amoeba, and therefore the two party system ceases to function. There were only two opinions, and only two groups to represent them, when the party system came into use. If there had been four parties in parliament at the time when the two party system of government was inaugurated, a four party system would have been introduced instead. To-day there are many parties, or groups, represented in parliament, and to continue to use a two party system in a four or six party legislature is like trying to build an industrial nation to-day with an ox-cart system of transportation, in despite of an up-to-date railway system.

The evolutionary principle recognizes a movement from the "indefinite" to the "definite," and from the "simple" to the "complex." Herbert Spencer in his "First Principles" traces the whole process with a thoroughness which carries conviction. He begins with the worlds in whirling orbs of fire, and ends with the human faculties as expressed in the highest art, showing that everywhere, and in everything, the universal law works from the simple to the complex, and from the indefinite to the definite. This evolutionary principle operates in the political realm just as it does in the physical, and that man is blind who cannot see it. " 'Tis true, 'tis pity, and pity 'tis, 'tis true"; the blind must be still many, for the failure to recognize this has brought both Canada and Great Britain to the verge of bloody revolution.

"Direct Action" is a phrase which has come to Canada with a new significance of late. What does it mean? And why has it come? It means that constitutional or political methods of achieving improvement have been given up as hopeless by a very large section of organized labor. Generations of fruitless effort have culminated in a repudiation of political governments as they are known, and the workers incline to use their industrial power in whichever way it will be most effective. There can be no doubt that this is a serious drift; organized industrial workers, although they may be only a small minority, can paralyse the nation by the use of the strike weapon, or by other similar weapons. But this unfortunate development has a cause. It does not appear by accident. What is the cause for the inclination to take direct action? The obvious cause is that, through the party system of government, and our method of voting, industrial groups have no means of expressing themselves. The voice of labor seldom reaches the legislative assembly. It is seldom that labor men have tried to elect representatives to parliament in Canada. The helplessness of a few labor or farmer members under the party system was discouraging enough, but the difficulty in electing them was even more discouraging. The present system of voting, which fits the party system well, together with the gerrymandering game of politicians, make it almost impossible to elect a labor member except in a very few constituencies. To send a labor man to parliament to-day he must be voted through an unorganized mass of middle-class stupidity. While labor represents a fair proportion of the votes of the country as a whole, yet the constituencies are so arranged as to leave labor in the minority in almost every riding; with the result that the wishes of the worker are never expressed. When the wage-earners have tried to elect men to parliament, some flimsy, trumped-up issue has always carried the ignorant unorganized mass, thus overwhelming the well-defined and expert opinion of an organized group. It is no wonder then that labor is tempted to bolt from the tracks of constitutionality. As things are, labor has little chance of obtaining adequate representation, and there can be no remedy for social unrest until labor is represented, its voice heard, and its grievances honestly faced in parliament. If proper provision is not made for giving expression politically to industrial organizations, we may have to suffer the penalty, in the form of open disregard of constituted authority. Organized industrial groups are everywhere refusing to give up the interests which brought them together, they are refusing to dilute their solidified opinions with unorganized mass notions, and in consequence group representatives are getting into parliament despite the disadvantages of the party system of voting.

There is no country in the civilized world that has only two parties. Europe long since has yielded to the complexity of group opinions. France might be instanced as a good example. At the last election in that country there were elected 117 Republicans left, 52 Radicals, 71 Radical Socialists, 24 Republican Socialists, 54 Unified Socialists, 6 Dissident Socialists, 120 Progressives, 76 L'Acton Group Liberel, and 31 Conservatives. In Great Britain there were seventeen groups seeking political representation in the election of 1918. South Africa has five groups of almost equal strength—the Nationalists, South African Party, Unionists, Labor, and Independents. In our Federal Government there are Tories, Grits, Unionists, Farmers, and Labor. In the provincial parliaments, there are, in Ontario, four groups, not one of which is strong enough to form a party government; Alberta has five groups, Tory, Liberal, Soldier, Farmer, and Labor, while a similar political manifestation is to be found in Manitoba, Saskatchewan, and British Columbia. In keeping with the evolutionary principle referred to, we are moving from the simple party division towards a more complex form of government that will reflect all organized opinion; and we are moving from the indefinite jelly formation of mass opinion, to the definite, solidified, and expert opinion of organized groups. Under these conditions the party system becomes obsolete.

The coming of groups into parliament is not a matter of theory, it is a fact. Conducting a government, in many parliaments to-day, with four groups, is a practical problem, and it is to be expected that the solution for the problem will be found in a group government which will give expression to all groups, and which will place equal responsibility upon all groups. To attempt to carry on with a two-party system, when there are four parties, will be both difficult and dangerous. As soon as a third party appears in parliament, there is danger of injustice, for if that third party can upset or embarrass the party in power, by combining with the opposition, it will refrain from doing so only when assured of concessions from the government. This means that a third party, or groups, under the two party system has much more influence in parliament than is consistent with justice and democracy. The third group or party may coerce a government into doing certain things by threatening to vote with the opposition; for a party government will do almost anything to save its skin, and avoid defeat. This danger is increased as the number of groups increases.

It would appear that the inevitable outcome will be the adoption of a nonpartisan, or group, form of government. As this will be dealt with later, it is sufficient to say here that the party system is being pushed out of existence by natural forces, and the challenge to every statesman is to adopt a form of government that will serve our time as effectively as the party system served an earlier, simpler society. Science, applied to industry, has led to the division of labor, and specialization; this in turn has led to industrial group organization based on particular group interests; these groups are seeking representation in parliaments; and once they get to parliament the two party system becomes inoperative, and some form of group government is necessary. In this way the party system will pass away, and a new form more suitable to modern conditions inevitably replace it.

CHAPTER II.

THE OUTLOOK OF THE NEW LEADERSHIP

Progress by At- traction. The perspective attempted in the foregoing chapter shows that what is really taking place is not a mere departmental reconstruction, but that society as a whole is being transformed. The war just ended is not responsible for the changes that are taking place; it but revealed social weaknesses in such a way as to attract to them the attention of the masses. But society is doing what it has always done, that is, accommodating itself to conditions. The various phases of human life, represented in what we call institutions, are so inter-related that any alteration of a fundamental character in one must, of necessity, affect all. So we see that in church and state, in industry and government, in every department, society is being remodelled upon a democratic and co-operative basis.

Contrary to what has been predicted by many thinkers, society will embrace the new social order without any cataclysmic upheaval. We are gradually growing towards it. The old cells are dropping off one by one, and new cells are being formed. The stability of society while in the process of reconstruction has already given confidence to the diffident, and paved the way for further progress. The fear of destruction has been allayed, and conservatism in itself has ceased to be a virtue.

It often occurs that those who aspire to leadership in progressive movements lay undue stress upon the destruction of what *is,* under the impression that violence against the existing order is a necessary preliminary to the establishment of that which progressives think *ought to be.* People generally regard the iconoclast, the destroyer, or terrorist, with grave misgiving, and are more afraid of the destroying process than attracted by what, it is alleged, will follow. The consequence is that reformers, in their impatience with slow development, and ardently desiring to bring about the state of affairs revealed in their prophetic vision, frequently set back the cause which they aim to advance.

But the idea of destruction as a means of progress is not confined to reformers; it has been advocated and practised, in so far as practice was possible, by the authorities of all time. Not only reformers, but those opposing reforms, when gripped by the fear of being destroyed, and bent chiefly on maintaining their own hold on social forces, have been among the most vigorous and immoderate advocates of destruction. Until there is some right thinking done in connection with this business of destroying, people will on the one hand fear it, and on the other attempt it.

As far as the idea of destruction is applied to social institutions, I believe it grows out of two misconceptions, i.e., a false analogy of society, and a failure to recognize the truth that nothing can be destroyed. Few reformers are able to see society as a whole; authorities in church and state, schooled in certain beliefs, seldom see the outsiders' point of view; and comparatively few people reach the plane of philosophy from which may be seen the eternal unity which threads diversity as the cord threads the necklace. The examination and analysis of parts have made them oblivious of the whole. The inter-relationship between the parts is lost sight of, to the exclusion of the completeness which characterizes common life.

Some see life as devolution, others as evolution; very few realize it as a phenomenon involving both processes. Some see life as a conflict, others as a co-operation; some see order, others chaos; some see an unfolding purpose, while to others, again, all is meaningless. By looking too long, or too closely, at a part, the part fills our field of vision and becomes all there is. If, as with a telescope, our vision takes in the perspective, we may see the proper relation of one part to another, and recognize that truth, full-orbed, is composed of all—struggle and co-operation both—and that in the whole these diverse elements find unity, so that, with Browning, we will say:

> Seek
> Full truth my soul may, when some babe I saw
> A new-born weakling, starts up strong—not weak—
> Not by foiled daring, fond attempts back driven;
> Fine faults of growth, brave sins which saint when
>   shriven—
> To stand full-statured in magnificence.

In the unity we see the connection between the new-born weakling and the full-statured magnificence. Meanwhile our partial vision, with our loyalties to the little that we do see, are "brave sins," "fine faults of growth."

When society is seen as a living organism developing in harmony with the laws of life, and not as something which politicians have put together, as it were, with hammer and nails, we shall cease to think of destruction, and use time and effort for the purpose of cultivation; we shall see that society, like the individual, is part of all it has met with—part of all it has experienced; imbedded in its being is all of the past, and that past, combined with the present, determines its future.

The indestructibility of anything that exists is an acknowledged fact of physical science. What passes for destruction with the superficial witness, however, is but the changing of form, or the passing from one state of existence to another. I maintain that this principle of indestructibility is no less true when applied to thought, or to the institutions of society, than it is in physics, and that, if this truth were fully realized, governments would no longer attempt by suppression and persecution to destroy new thoughts and new systems; neither would radicals act as though old systems should be attacked and destroyed in order to make way for new. Nature is working in the thought and action departments of human life as accurately and as firmly as she works in the physical universe. Destruction is not one of nature's methods. She has provided against the possibility of destroying. The old system will change its form under the proper natural conditions without the aid of iconoclasm.

It is, perhaps, discouraging that human history has failed to teach this lesson more widely, especially as it is written on every page. In all ages futility has marked the course of those who have attempted to extirpate ideas by force. It always was so, and always will be. But not yet is this sufficiently realized. The government of Canada, particularly during the great war, brought into use the outworn, senseless methods of suppression, notwithstanding the fact that history fails to give us one instance in which the effort to club ideas has been successful. Clubs, it is true, may kill the individual with the idea, but nothing spreads ideas so far, or so quickly, as the blood of the oppressed. Constituted authorities, fearing that something held by them to be of value will be destroyed, make the fatal mistake of molesting those advocating that which they fear. This applies chiefly to matters of religion and political economy. But no one is afraid that the explorer will upset gravity when he starts on an expedition; nor does anyone fear that the physical laws of the universe will be violated when the scientist enters his laboratory. Why, then, should politicians fear the opinion of sociologists, or even the ruddiest utterances of the rosiest "reds"? The laws of society are just as well protected by nature as any other laws in existence. If we go back in history a little, we will find Bruno burned to death by authorities because he tried to establish the idea that the world we inhabit was shaped like a ball. But the burning of Bruno did not make the world flat. In spite of fire—here or hereafter—it obstinately remained round. Being round, sooner or later it was *seen* to be round; until in the end, what Bruno once saw, all see, and his persecution is condemned as the stupid thing it was. So it is with all things. Love was not lost to the world when the world's greatest Lover was crucified; neither will the ideas for which I am contending in this book perish with the disappearance of a few of those who hold them.

Our governments are taking the club method to-day. Bolshevism, the O.B.U., strikes, agitators, publications, all must be suppressed by fines, threats, imprisonments, and deportations. Now, I am neither defending nor condemning Bolshevism, nor the O.B.U., nor strikes. All I want to say is that repressive methods will not prevail against these things if the laws of society justify them. If the laws of society do not call for the uprisings and revolutions which the governments dread, neither agitators nor revolutionists can bring them about. The iron laws of society are stronger than the temporary laws of politicians.

Faith in truth is what the world requires. No one needs to fear except, perhaps, those who live by privileges which truth does not sanction. A nation with faith in truth will never have political prisoners, nor obscurantism, nor suppression of speech. It will know that truth cannot be destroyed.

Every reformer should abolish the term "destruction" from his vocabulary. Not only has it no place in scientific thinking, but it makes people afraid. People are not attracted by a program of destruction, and yet people must be attracted and won if substantial reforms are to be attained. Somehow, the advocates of reform in the last generation or two have put a great deal more emphasis upon the necessity of getting rid of the old than they have put on the desirability of the new. Naturally, the result is that people are fearful when they should be confident, and those opposed to reforms exploit this fear as a means of retarding progress.

The challenge which comes to every leader in new thoughts and new methods comes from truth itself. Truth knows nothing of destruction, and says to those entrusted with her cause, "If you are a destroyer, you do not know me." The attractiveness of any movement is of greater importance than the defects in that which it is intended to supersede, and should not be defaced by misrepresentation. Every person espousing a cause must feel and accept some responsibility for the proper interpretation of that cause. To spread abroad misrepresentation is to create distrust, and those guilty of so doing are hinderers, not helpers, and when distrust has, in this or any other way, been created; then it is that truth has been wounded in the house of her friends, and needs to be saved from them.

Organizations or movements are seldom in danger of being permanently defeated by outside opposition. It is true that external opposition retards progress, but it will never be successful in forcing ultimate defeat on any movement that is founded on necessity. The opinion is trite which holds that the greatest enemies and the most dangerous to any cause are those within. Those within are the greatest enemies because the movement is judged by their mistakes, and because when they act unwisely, they do so with the genuine enthusiasm of sincerity.

Movements are often misrepresented by opponents, but no cause for this should be given by responsible advocates. The proper introduction to every gospel is, "We come that ye might have life, and that ye might have it more abundantly," and "We come, not to destroy, but to fulfil." What chance has anyone, or what chance should anyone have, who comes to destroy? They who come to destroy come to do the impossible. They are defeated before they begin. Even when they appeared confidently, with a message of good-will on their lips, and in their hearts, great teachers have been crucified, and, sad to think, must still appear, and still be dealt with in the same treacherous way that their predecessors were.

Great achievements have been accepted, in the past, because of their attractiveness. People select, naturally, that which serves their highest purpose best, and in this respect political or industrial systems are no different. If shown to be serviceable, people will desire them.

Whoever would achieve in social reformation would do well to take a hint from politicians and those who have been successful in commercial enterprises. If politicians sought votes for what they intended to do, they would receive none. They obtain votes because they promise good things. The lesson is that people are looking for good things. This fact is commercialized and degraded by politicians, and often ignored by reformers. Commercial enterprise is successful, because it promises service to people. As soon as confidence is established, success is secure.

When the first railroad was built, the promoters did not send speakers throughout the country asking people to break up all wagons and carts, and shoot the horses; or advocating the destruction of highways and footpaths because a new method of transportation had been devised. No! The railroad was built, and people stopped transportation by means of wagons, and shipped their freight by rail because to ship by rail was advantageous. Nor yet when telegraphy was discovered, did the promoters advocate the destruction of the postal system; they strung a wire along poles, and, of its own value, their achievement superseded the postal system in business enterprise.

Reformers, to be successful, must be able to give the positive presentation of their case. Instead of saying: "Upset the government," "Down with capital," "To hell with the System," etc., they must say: "We come to fulfil the highest functions of these." Capital must be used to greater advantage for the common good; it must be made to serve. Capitalists will not be destroyed; they will be called to the higher service of managing capital for national well-being; and governments will be fulfilled in being made to represent the people truly, and to manage with honesty and efficiency the public business. The philosophy of the new social order is positive, constructive, and fulfilling. It brings the more abundant life as well to those who have as to those who have not. Truth demands that we redeem our social aspirations from disgruntled negations to a positive gospel of hope, capable of inspiring confidence.

"Truth," if it be "lifted up," will draw all people unto it. The world will follow when we can show a better way. It is the privilege and duty of organized farmers to show the better way in politics and industry. They do not come to destroy political parties. All parties are alike to them. The farmers come to do more honestly, more democratically, and more efficiently, that which the old parties have been

97

trying to do. In their economic oppression and political wandering, the farmers have discovered the new law and the new hope. They do not seek to destroy, but to fulfil, governments; they do not want to compete with the exploiters for the lion's share of the plunder, but seek true co-operation in all things for the highest common good.

With such an outlook, the method of campaigning should be to educate and guide. There are too many people with good intentions who try to take the world by the throat. The farmers aim to take the world by the hand, and in the spirit of co-operation go forward into the new day together.

§2

The New Leaders The foregoing survey of what may be called the main factors of civilization reveals that there is at present a great ferment and agitation in all departments of society. The unrest, which may be taken as symptomatic of the approaching era, is not confined to one phase of national life; it is all-pervasive and universal. All institutions are in the ever-moving current of progress, and there is nothing to be feared unless there is tampering with natural laws. The only danger comes from those who would seek by artificial means to retard progress. As well might one try to stop the river with a dam. All that happens in such a case is that the force is stored up until it equals the resistance of the barrier, and then the water rushes wildly over, carrying all before it in hopeless confusion. The effect of every restriction of, or repressive act against, social unrest, on the part of public officials, is exactly similar. Sane direction, not autocratic repression, is what is needed to-day more than anything else.

The world outlook is social. Individualism is passing out, co-operation is coming in, and everything must be adjusted to the change.

New times demand new measures and new men;
The world advances, and in time outgrows
The laws that in our fathers' day were best;
And doubtless, after us, some purer scheme
Will be shaped out by wiser men than we,
Made wiser by the steady growth of truth.

"New men" as well as "new measures" are needed. Those who were the most efficient in individualism will be, for that very reason, the most inefficient under co-operation. Most of our leaders in industry, religion, education, and government, are not qualified for leadership in a new social order. No matter how well intentioned they may be, their whole training is against them. They belong to yesterday. It will be seen that most leaders to-day are followers, and not only followers, but they are as a rule "following afar off,"—much too far off as a matter of fact to allow us to entertain much hope of them. They hanker after the past, do not see the new dawn, and lack the courage to take the initiative. Objectionable as it may be to some, the new leaders are coming from the ranks of those who have been up till now the "despised and rejected of men." The agrarian and urban industrial organizations are the Nazareth from which are coming the prophets of a new day.

. . . . . A time like this demands
Strong minds, great hearts, true faith, and willing hands.

In response to the yearning expressed in these lines, honest toilers from the factory, with a devotion to justice, with a reverence for everything human, and with an indomitable courage to act, are assuming the responsibilities that have been considered, heretofore, the special prerogatives of the aristocracy; and the farmer, like Cincinnatus of old, is leaving his plow for the legislative halls. These are the "new men." To those who doubt the reality of the new Nazareth, I say, "Come and see."

OUTLOOK OF THE NEW LEADERSHIP

The United Farmers' movement in Canada took its rise in the general environment of unrest I have described. The more immediate economic environment leading to the organization of the agrarian workers will be considered in detail, later. But the atmosphere of progressive ideas into which the United Farmers organization was born has had more than a passing significance in shaping the ideals and destiny of the movement. Born in due time, nurtured in unrest, and breathing as the very breath of life the universal spirit of Justice, the United Farmers of Canada are in a position to give that service to the nation which at this time it sorely needs. The farmers are in a position to do great national service, not only because they awoke to consciousness in the midst of a changing world, but also because their aims are synthetic. Although fathered by oppression, the farmers' movement has escaped that bitterness of feeling against capital, and that extreme rashness both of expression and action, so characteristic of labor. The farmer, in reality, combines in his own profession, the two antagonists. He is both capitalist and laborer. He knows that production is not furthered when war is going on between the two. He sees, also the hopeless

PART TWO

THE ORIGIN AND DEVELOPMENT OF THE UNITED FARMERS' MOVEMENT

CHAPTER I.

ECONOMIC NECESSITY

§1

Why the Farmers Organized. How did the farmers' organization originate? Did it spring into being over night, or did it grow in spontaneous response to conditions? The answer to these questions will furnish us with the key to the proper interpretation of the movement. The general environment of the movement has already been given. Its character has been affected by the atmosphere of unrest, and the universal desire for social justice peculiar to the period. We have now to examine the more immediate economic environment in which the United Farmers' organization took its rise. To do this thoroughly would mean writing a complete history of the movement, which cannot, of course, in this place, even be attempted. I would rather refer the reader to "Deep Furrows" by Mr. Hopkins Moorhouse. In that excellent work will be found the history of the men and conditions that combined to make the agrarian outlook what it is to-day. But it is imperative that we review some of the economic factors that have served to force the Canadian farmers out of their individualism, and made them join hands in the cause of their own self-preservation.

It may seem strange to some to mention land monopoly as one of the injustices which, indirectly, led to organized protest on the part of the farmers, but nevertheless, the land question is of fundamental importance.   There is so much land in Canada that, at this early stage of our history, to speak of a land problem at all will appear to be ridiculous.   The patriotic politician in his flight of eloquence concerning the boundless and immeasurable resources of this country, we have all heard.   He never fails to dilate on the millions of acres of virgin soil more fertile than Eden of old, waiting to pour its rich harvests into the bins of merry ploughmen.   Alas! half truths are worse than lies. True the land is here, true it is fertile, but it is not waiting for the ploughmen, it is waiting for the "price"; and that price is fixed by the speculator; it is the chief barrier between the merry ploughmen and those "rich harvests" of the politicians' dream.   Certainly Canada has rich soil and extensive natural resources, but these resources do not belong to Canada; they are owned by individuals, many of whom do not even live in Canada. It is no secret that the heritage of millions of Canadian children yet unborn has been given away to individuals, railroads, and land companies. Children read the story of the Forty Thieves with excited interest; but the story of Canadian resources in their relation to twenty-three money kings, which is equally exciting, has been tabooed. It should be made the basis of Canadian history. If in our Sunday schools it is considered wise and religious to teach the children how the land of Canaan was divided among the Israelites, it would surely not be out of place to let them know how Canada has been divided among the plutocrats.

In a country so rich in natural resources poverty should be unknown. Canada has an area of 1,401,316,413 acres. Of this 440,951,000 acres are arable, while only 36,000,000 acres are under cultivation. There are 170,000,000 acres of timber land, bearing approximately 700,000,-000,000 feet. Our coal deposits are conservatively estimated at 1,234,269,000,000 tons. There are also rich deposits of iron, nickel, gold, and other minerals. The water power of

Canada, which is another valuable asset, is calculated to be 17,746,000 horse power. The soil is as rich as any in the world, and produces abundantly all kinds of grain, grasses, vegetables, and fruits. The abundance of Canada's natural resources is beyond computation, and is still practically untouched. The population is small. If all the homes in Canada were placed in such a way as to cover the whole area, allowing the same area of land for each, they would be so far apart as to be out of sight of each other. Yet with one of the smallest populations in one of the largest and richest countries in the world, poverty abounds.

A life insurance company recently advertised that "amongst every thousand men who reach sixty-five there are four hundred dependents upon private or public charity." In 1915 the daily press of Winnipeg reported that there were four thousand children, in that city alone, whose parents were too poor to provide any Christmas festivities. In 1901 there were in Canada 46,154 families living in single rooms and in 1910 the number of families living in single rooms had increased to 80,702.

Poverty is not confined to the cities. Its dreadful shadow is everywhere on the great fertile Canadian plains. It is produced through the monopoly of natural resources, and by the exploitation of the agrarian toilers. A glance at a few of the facts will suffice to demonstrate the truth of the statement. In the three prairie provinces there are 153,000,000 acres of tillable land, of which 16,000,000 acres only are cultivated, while 100,000,000 acres are held by speculators. Thousands of people, many of whom are returned soldiers, desire to use this land and production would be enormously increased if it were available to these people for use. But the prices charged by the speculators are prohibitive, and, as a matter of unexaggerated fact, most purchasers of land under the present unfavorable agricultural conditions simply bind themselves to slave their lives away for mortgage companies.

One of the largest land holders in the prairie provinces is the Canada Northwest Land Co., Ltd., whose board of directors is practically that of the Canadian Pacific Railway Co. In addition to an interest in the Canadian Pacific Railway townsites, this company owns 373,165 acres. The Canadian Northern Prairie Lands Co., under Canadian Northern Railway direction, holds 67,319 acres; the Hudson's Bay Co. has

4,058,050 acres; and the Canadian Northern Railway Co. owns 6,511,394 acres. The Canadian Pacific Railway Co. has been selling its land for twenty years or more. By the sale of 21,000,000 acres the company realized over $100,000,000.

Much of the land now under cultivation has been purchased by farmers from these privileged companies. This, together with the tariff, the high freight rates, and the low price of wheat, accounts for the fact that a large percentage of the farmers are operating to-day under the gentle care of mortgage companies. In Saskatchewan it is estimated that eighty per cent. of all farm lands is mortgaged, and a similar condition of things exists in the other Canadian provinces.

The homestead policy can scarcely be said to have been devised either in the interests of agriculture, or of the homesteaders themselves. It was devised in the interests of railroads and land companies. Settlers were necessary to the country if the land values were to be improved, and if the railroads were to be profitable, and hence the free homesteads offered as alluring inducement. But these homesteads were not of the best lands; the best had already been picked; neither were they close to the railway, for land adjacent to the railroads had been disposed of already; and so the homestead farmer suffered from land monopoly from the very first. Forced to go anywhere from five to forty miles from a railroad, the pioneer lost by the increased cost of the production of his marketable commodities. He spent more time on the road, used more horses, and wore out more wagons. But he had also to build roads from his lonely homestead, over, and through, miles of unused land, much of which was untaxable. Schools, too, had to be supported, and the price of land kept settlers away, so that the burden fell more heavily on the small community. As time went on these pioneer farmers had built roads and established schools; small towns sprang up, and the land values created by the social toil of these people were added to the price of the exploiter's land. Farmers who came after the homestead lands were taken up were forced to pay to railway companies and land companies the values created by the toil of their fellow farmers. This was a burden which handicapped the later settlers, even though, by buying the land of the speculators, they were nearer to the railroads than the pioneers. And so in both cases, in the case of the first settlers on account of the extra work entailed, and in the case of the later settlers on account of the high prices paid for land, the cost of production was increased to that point where there was practically nothing left for the farmer except a bare existence. Unlike the manufacturer, you see, the farmer could not add the increased cost of production to the selling price of wheat, or beef, or whatever it was he produced on his farm; the prices were set—both ways—and all he could do was to pay what was asked, and take what was given, and still "keep smiling."

It was the greed of the land and natural resources exploiters that led to the building of the transcontinental lines of railroad. Instead of concentrating our railway system in that part of the Dominion that was already settled, and instead of developing the natural resources by which they were surrounded, for the national benefit, these resources were grabbed up everywhere, from coast to coast, and a railway was run across thousands of miles of waste like an ostrich track in a desert. It is safe to say that the population of Canada could all be concentrated in one province like Ontario, without suffering from over-crowding, and the railways which were necessary to span the Dominion, had they

been built on a plan governed by the requirements of the case, would have given greater service at infinitely less expense. As it was, although our railroads were built by the people,
according to the exploiters' idea of development, they resulted in a most costly undertaking,
giving a minimum of service. Freight rates
had to be raised so as to cover the extravagance
in construction, and this fell upon the shoulders
of the farmers, more than upon any other class.
The farmer lost the price of freight on the selling
price of his wheat, and had to pay the freight on
all machinery and other commodities necessary
to his life on the farm.

In addition to the enormous gifts of land to
railroads, they received from the Canadian people in actual cash $244,000,000, besides guaran-
teed bonds to the value of $245,000,000. All
this notwithstanding, the people of Canada did
not own the Canadian railways. This is proved
by the fact that latterly some of them, after having become bankrupt, have been bought again
by public money, presumably in order to save
the investments made by the magnates in control. Consequently, while our railway schemes
necessitated high freights, the greed of profit
made the freights higher still, all of which in-

creased the burdens of the farmer, and made them heavier than they were.

The tariff, which has long been recognized by a large section of the people as a social crime, constitutes another of the economic prods which served to drive the farmers into co-operation. This subject has been so much talked about, and its injustice is so obvious that I need but to mention it. The tariff crime, sometimes committed in the sacred name of patriotism, at other times excused as a producer of revenue, and invariably represented to the workers as the salvation of their jobs, stands as one of the most glaring examples of class legislation which the history of Canada affords. Industries claimed that they needed protection on the grounds that they could not compete with manufacturers of the United States and Great Britain. This protection was granted because the financial interests engaged in manufacture controlled the government.

The farmers had to raise wheat, and sell it on the world's market for the current price, and in doing so the Canadian farmer was, and is, handicapped. There are natural disadvantages such as drought, hail, frost, rust, smut, hot winds, and so on, and numerous artificial ones, the long hauls, for instance, and their consequent high freight rates. Many of these difficulties are not found in other wheat-raising countries, hence while it is not easy for the Canadian farmer to compete with other countries, yet he has done it, and is continuing to do it, without protection. If the farmer, in the face of so many difficulties, gets no protection, and asks none, why should manufacturers be protected at the expense of the farmer, thus making it next to impossible for that which is the basic industry of the country to exist? This thought came to the farmers, as sooner or later it was bound to come, and the longer he thought the plainer it became that the injustices of land and tariff monopolies under which he suffered, together with the many other tyrannies, high freights, etc., were slowly encroaching on his very life, threatening his existence, and if he would continue to live it was necessary that he should do something in his own behalf, do it without delay, and do it himself.

There came a time when the pressure of these injustices became so severe that farmers had to give up their land and move to the cities in order to be able to live. Then people began to wonder and talk and speculate on the reason why the farmers had left their farms. Some said that farmers who gave up and went to the city were lazy, others said it was the gaiety of city life that lured them. The farmer alone knew that the exodus was due to economic necessity. Manufacturers, railroad magnates, real estate dealers, and governments began a "Back to the Land" campaign, without making the slightest attempt to solve the problem which accounted for the vacant farms, without even understanding for the most part that such a problem existed. Perhaps it is one of the tragedies of our society that those responsible for much of the trouble are entirely unconscious of it.

Meanwhile the farmers, now alive to the necessity for sane action on their part, began to watch their oppressors. They saw that while they were themselves standing as individuals, in political and economic helplessness, the industrial magnates were organized, and through organization were able to dominate. They saw that through organization the banks were able to say how much they would charge for money, the manufacturers how much was to be paid for their manufactured article, the railroads how much was to be charged for freight; the land owner fixed the price of his land, and even the laborers were getting together and demanding a price for their labor. So the farmers said: "We, too, will organize, and see if by that means we cannot decide ourselves what shall be paid for wheat, instead of leaving it to be decided by wheat dealers as we have done for so long."

This is, in brief, the economic history of the farmers' movement. Involved in this, from the pioneer period until the present time, are struggles, deprivations, and defeats, which will never be known. But out of it all was born and developed that self-confidence which brought the farmers to the point where they resolved to become their own emancipators. Economically crushed and politically befooled, bedevilled by politicians who were the henchmen of privilege, with the fields of their political hope strewn with the broken promises of parties and governments, and with confidence in autocracy utterly shattered, the farmers came to the conclusion that they must protect themselves by organization, and were ultimately led to see in cooperation the philosophy of a new and better age. Deep in the soil of economic oppression are the roots of the farmers' organization. It took form spontaneously and grew; but grew, not like the mushroom, but like the mighty oak, strong and durable.

THE FARMERS IN POLITICS

§2

The United Farm Women. The organization of the farm women is of equal importance with that of the farmers themselves. The United Farmers' movement, as we have seen, sprang directly from economic conditions. Its counterpart—the United Farm Women—although seemingly inspired to action from somewhat different motives, is no less dependent on and concerned with economics and politics. In our civilization it has been considered the prerogative of men to provide the necessities of life for the family. For this reason women have been removed one step at least from the actual scene of economic conflict, and perhaps have been in the past prone to attribute any scarcity or hardship, met with in the family life, to the improvidence of the husband, rather than to the economic system to which it was due. If then we find that women to-day in general tend to emphasize what is usually called the spiritual side of life rather than the material, it is not that they do not recognize the fundamental character of material things, but that, on the one hand, they still feel it to be the particular business of *men* to attend to economic concerns, while, on the other, the environment of the home, conditioned as it is by the economic struggle, is more congenial to moral impulse than business life. The United Farmers' organization stood as a breakwater upon which the fury of the sea was expended. But when the tidal waves of economic distress threatened to demolish the home, in spite of the breakwater, the guardians of the home—the mothers—were not long in jumping to the aid of their husbands in strengthening the defence. In other words, the farm women very soon found out that they could not make the rural home that place of beauty and happiness they desired, nor protect it against the hardships and evils which beset it, unless the economic conditions were altered, and so they were led to join forces with the men in the field of political conflict with a view to securing economic emancipation as the first step toward better living conditions. But they brought with them those influences pertaining to idealism which were necessary to give proper balance to the farmers' movement as a whole, and thus became a true and valuable complement.

The women of the farms are already in the front rank of the progressive movement. They did not begin to organize until 1910, yet they have already become a powerful factor in Canadian national life. The extension of the franchise to women has increased their influence tremendously. Before this was granted, legislators paid but little attention to their expressed desires, and none at all to those that were unexpressed. Now, however, having the vote, and—what is of even greater value—being organized in such a way as to use it intelligently, the farm women are beginning to be recognized. Their executives are consulted on legislation, and their convention resolutions give the cue to political platform makers.

As compared with city women, farm women, in preparing themselves for active participation in matters of public concern, are at a decided disadvantage. Nevertheless it seems that in respect of that fuller life after which humanity is reaching to-day, they are in the van. One has but to consult the year books of the various provincial associations, or to follow the deliberations of their conventions, to discover that in education, health, home life, the development of the young and preparation of them for the greater responsibilities of citizenship, and in raising the moral standard, the women of the farms are taking the leadership. There are doubtless many contributing causes for this outstanding radical aggressiveness on the part of rural women's organizations. Perhaps chief among these is the fact that women on the farms have in the past suffered enormously from lack of just such things as healthy social intercourse, a community spirit, opportunities for their children along educational and recreational lines, and more than all else, for lack of proper medical attention, or even medical attention of any kind. The actual urgency arising out of the conditions of life in rural Canada has helped to awaken the mothers especially to accept the responsibility for the health, development, and happiness of their communities. Farm women have little time and less inclination for the frivolities which occupy the attention of many "society" women. The mothers on the farms are grappling with real life problems, and their struggle against gigantic odds, during many years of pioneering, has been noble and heroic in the extreme. It is natural, therefore, that their present efforts should have high and exceptional value. They are washing the powder and paint off the face of a sham society, and replacing it with the beauty of nature and reality.

It is true that the great and difficult task of

organizing the farm women is but just begun; and still more true that the issues and measures now being discussed, must pass into legislation and be properly administered before rural life will approximate the ideals of the United Farm Women. But, even so, their ability to take part in working out national problems is marked, and their average intelligence high. A large percentage of our population, particularly in the western provinces, came from the British Isles, and from the United States. They had a fair education, and in addition that culture which comes through mingling with people of different nationalities, and were therefore, prospectively, citizens of a high type. Then, a large proportion of the Canadian born women on the farms were well educated. Many of them were school teachers who linked up their lives with those of the Western homesteaders, and are now in a position to take the leadership in one of the greatest movements in the history of Canada. Not only, then, do the United Farm Women possess the ability, but, as well, they have the courage to take the initiative. It was a farm women, Mrs. L. C. McKinney, of Claresholm, Alberta, who was the first woman in the whole of the British Empire to occupy a seat in a legislature. Since her election there have been other women elected to parliament, both in Great Britain and in Canada; and the more the appreciation of human values as against commercial values becomes general, the more the need for women members of parliament will be recognized, and the more women members will we have.

The Farm Women's organization is, properly speaking, a section of the United Farmers' movement. Although there are two organizations, the movement is one. There are two bodies because the men and the women approached the same problems from different angles. As I have shown, the farmers' organization was primarily economic in origin and aim. In the earlier stages, it did not see much beyond the price of wheat, the lowering of freight rates, and the abolition of the tariff. But men, in their struggle against the evils of commercialism, have been commercialized, and the farmer is no exception to the rule. Plutocratic organizations are dominated by the desire for higher profit, labor organizations concentrate on higher profit labor organizations concentrate on higher wages, and farmer organizations, too, began by seeking higher prices. Legislation, also, during the whole period of women's enslavement, has been materialistic, and commercial. What the world has lost by the exclusion of women from participation in industry, commerce, and politics, will never be known, but we obtain a hint of the nature of humanity's loss, owing to this unfortunate exclusion of women, from their contribution so far, and while their freedom is only dawning. The United Farm Women have helped greatly to save the United Farmers' movement from the usual fate of male movements. The male mind, during the individualistic system of society, went to seed on commercialism; and the human values, such as character, the development of the aesthetic tastes, and the desire for the highest happiness, have been choked out.

It cannot be truthfully denied that economic questions are fundamental. The first question to every person is, "How am I to live?" But that is not the only question. There is another and an even greater, "Why am I living?" If one has to live merely to secure bread in order to live while more bread is secured, then death is preferable to life. But "How am I to live?" is still, and must remain, the first question. If an answer is not found to this, answer to the second there can be none. Without bread one does not make enquiries about that for which one *should* live. These questions have produced two schools of thought, one the materialistic, the other the idealistic, and much of the world's time and energy is being wasted in a conflict which is based largely on abstractions. Obviously, both outlooks belong to life. The one has no meaning without the other. If life is to continue, its means of existence must first be secured. Hence the importance of school number one. But having been secured, if progress is to be made, happiness must take precedence of mere means of existence. The emphasis therefore is placed by school number two on this latter problem. But it is artificial to distinguish between life itself and life worth while. The materialistic and idealistic schools must be brought together and unified on a basis that will uphold life as a whole.

Economics is of first importance because one must eat to live, but one cannot live on ideals. The economic struggle itself, however, must find its justification in that for which people are living. It is very doubtful if the purely bread-and-butter man exists. People do not respond to a bread-and-butter appeal unless starvation stares them in the face. In the absence of bread-and-butter, bread-and-butter, of course, *is* the ideal. Necessities, however, once secured, it then becomes true that man does not live by bread alone; *but not until then.* It is chiefly for this reason that Marxian Socialism, as frequently misrepresented, has met with small success. But while man refuses to live for bread alone, he does not blindly follow the fantastic word pictures of those who ignore the most pressing facts of life. The failure of extreme materialistic radicalism as well as the failure of the orthodox church may safely be attributed to an over-emphasis on parts, and a failure to see the whole of life. The church has ignored the problem of getting a living, while the materialistic, so-called, has ignored the problem of *why* we should live. The United Farmers, happily, find a synthesis for the seeming antagonism between these two philosophies. They begin with the price of wheat, but they do not stop at that. Due mainly to the influence of the women's section, they have moved into a larger world of thought and action, where it is not only possible to live, but to make life worth the living.

The farm women approached modern problems from the viewpoint of obtaining a fuller life. The loneliness of the farm, lack of social and intellectual intercourse, the disadvantages of isolated homes, combined to bring the farm women together. Before that was done there was no means of developing a community spirit. Community life was hindered rather than helped by such organizations as existed up till that time. Even the churches tended to divide, instead of to unite it. The great need was to find a means of bringing all people together, regardless of religious belief, nationality, or political bias. Party political organization, together with denominationalism in the churches, stood in the way of undertaking community tasks. There were many things that might be improved by co-operative effort—phases and branches of life left entirely untouched by such organizations as were in existence. There were the young without healthy recreation or well directed amusement, and without education in vital matters. The youth of the farm was growing up, and growing more and more discontented. The lack of social life, and the difficulty in finding expression for youthful impulses, were even harder to bear than poverty in material things, and so the young people were drifting to the cities. To remedy this state of affairs was the work which the United Farm Women undertook first. They began to meet together in order to break the monotony and drudgery of the farm. Their organization was a revolt against the drab existence which was their lot. Their aim was to improve conditions as much as possible under the present political and economic systems, and was, therefore, from its inception, constructive and positive.

Meeting together in a social capacity soon led to a wider vision. Through fellowship the old barriers were broken down; there was an interchange and interpenetration of thought which developed the mind; the organization itself became not only a means of social intercourse and education, but a working apparatus that undertook and did things for community improvement. "It would require little organization," says Mrs. John McNaughton, "to get the majority of women to hold up their hands in favor of various measures of social and economic reform, but it takes a live organization to encourage its members to get out and help put these reforms into effect, and to see that they are properly administered."

ECONOMIC NECESSITY

"Underlying the women's section of the farmers' movement," says Mrs. Walter Parlby, who is one of the leaders, "is the thought that rural life rightly developed is the ideal life." The natural environment of the average rural home is thought to be such as will lead to the highest human development and enjoyment, providing that the advantages of civilization can also be enjoyed. There must, however, be time for leisure, and opportunity for education; the domestic conveniences enjoyed in the city must be brought to the farm; and proper care of health, including medical attention, must also be found for the rural communities. Such activities as tend toward the preservation of life, and lead to preparation for a fuller enjoyment of what it may yield—these are the things which, in the main, have occupied the attention of the United Farm Women.

Education, health, and work among the young people, with a view to making life worth while on the farm, have been specific objectives. For improvement in rural education the United Farm Women have advocated, and in many instances helped to make practicable, such reforms as making the school a community center; ob-

9

taining facilities for a resident teacher; beauti-
fying the school and school grounds; the cultivation of school gardens; the introduction of the
hot noon lunch; organized and supervised play;
school fairs and field days; and the changing of
the curriculum so as to make it more suitable to
the needs of rural children.

The future of the farmers' movement, like that
of all other movements, depends upon the rising
generation. In encouraging the formation of
junior branches of the United Farmers' organization, the women are doing essential and lasting
work. The aim in connection with the juniors
is to train the youths in citizenship; to make
agriculture a scientific profession, and to establish business efficiency on the farms; and in doing this it is proposed to follow a fourfold plan
of development which is educational, vocational,
economic, and social.

Watering stock in a huge business enterprise
is different from watering stock on the farm.
The business of farming is peculiar to itself, and
requires special training. The women's organization was quick to perceive the unregarded
needs of rural youths at school, and with the aid
of the extension departments of the Universities

is successfully meeting the requirements of young people through the junior department branch.

Health comes next on the program. I have but to mention the efforts put forth in this work to indicate its comprehensive nature. There has been strong agitation for municipal hospitals and these are about to be established. Medical inspection of schools has to some extent been secured, and will soon, it is hoped, become general. But there still remain municipal doctors, home nursing and first aid, child welfare, rural sanitation, prohibition, the care of delinquent and dependent children and of the mentally defective, to occupy the attention of the organization, and it is with such objects as these that it busies itself. "While the United Farm Women recognize the economic necessity underlying the movement as a whole," as Mrs. Leona Barritt says, "they are more directly interested in good homes, efficient schools, a healthy public spirit, wholesome recreation and amusement, and the education of the young people." Or, to put it Mrs. S. V. Haight's way, "The United Farmers fight for markets and finance, the United Farm Women for health, education, and morals."

But it is interesting to note how the farm women have been brought by their circuitous route face to face with economics, and also how the United Farmers, influenced by the women's viewpoint, have developed interest in many things other than the purely economic. The tariff and child welfare are both discussed now at the same convention.

There is not much doubt in the minds of the farm women about the economic problem. They know that, before it is solved, the higher things of life cannot be attained. They discovered the economic difficulty in the way of their obtaining a fuller and higher life. The farm women have approached economics from an angle much the same as that of John Ruskin or that of William Morris. These men loved life and beauty. They saw the world of human affairs from the artist's view. They wanted loveliness and harmony. In society they saw a hideous monster, and human relationships to them were nothing but a jarring discord. Ruskin and Morris sought the cause of this ugliness and found it. It was economic injustice, and this they bent all their energies to remove, not that they might get bread and butter, but that they might find beauty and truth. Similarly, the organized farm women have discovered that beautiful and happy homes, education, health, and the numerous other details of a complete life depend largely on economic conditions, and that the altering of economic conditions implies an intelligent interest in politics.

I take one example from the U.F.A. program, and trace it to its fulfilment in economics. The United Farm Women are interested in preparing themselves for the responsibilities of democratic citizenship. This presupposes a little leisure, and opportunity to read and think, and to take active part in democratic organization. How is that time to think to be found? Household economy must yield it. But the work in the home is a continual drudgery. So much is this the case that a speaker in a U.F.W. convention in describing it referred to certain "truthful tombstones" which said, "Jane scrubbed herself into eternity," and another, "Grandma washed herself away." But why is household work such drudgery? Because the household improvements of modern times are not everywhere available. Lighting plants, water and sewage systems, and machinery for doing many household duties are necessary but not accessible. Not only are these expensive, but new houses suitable for modern applications of household economy would have to be built. The problem is, how to obtain them; where are they to come from? "We have them not, but yet we see thee still." All this has a relation to the price of wheat. So we see that the very first step, time to think, leads by a circuitous path to economics, as do all the other steps proposed by the United Farm Women.

Political action, therefore, with a view to removing that economic injustice which prohibits the fullest life, is becoming an essential part of the woman's program. It may be expected that the influence upon politics of women in general will be similar to the influence of the United Farm Women on the farmers' movement. However that may be, the farmer and his partner stand shoulder to shoulder in the great political and economic struggle that is ahead, and it will take more than the ordinary political methods to beguile them from the path of freedom.

CHAPTER II.

DEMOCRACY AND THE GROUP

§1

The Chain of Social Progress. The United Farmers' movement, as I have said, is the result of the operation of economic and social laws. It was not planned in detail by any individual; and what it shall be is yet obscure. It has already branched out into educational, industrial, commercial, and political activities, but its future or the future of any or all of these departments cannot be previsioned with absolute accuracy; it will keep on, unfolding and accommodating itself to the laws by which it came into being and through which it exists. Apart from the laws of social progress the movement cannot be understood, but through a knowledge of the laws of society its inevitability will be seen, and the course of its drift may be noted with interest and advantage. By saying that the movement is the result of economic and social laws it is implied that it was born of necessity. It may quite truthfully be said that the farmers were *forced* to organize. To refuse to do so was to court dangers they were not prepared to face. We have already seen that specific economic conditions led directly to organized effort on the part of the farmers. We must now discover the laws which were in operation to produce the movement. They are not new laws, they are as old as the race. The advantages to be gained in referring to these laws are, first, that by them the movement will be seen in the chain of social progress, and inseparable from the general progress being made by society as a whole; and next, that those who oppose the movement may see that they are not dealing with whims and fancies, but with realities brought into being and directed by inevitable forces.

That social phenomena are the result of laws operating in society, as irrevocable in their nature and certain in their result as the laws of the physical world, is a truth as yet unrecognized not only by the masses, but by many individuals who claim the ability to expound social subjects. Social and economic laws cannot be ignored with impunity any more than we can ignore gravity by walking off the house top into the air. The laws that operate in human society must be discovered, studied, and utilized, in the interests of social progress. Man has conquered the physical world not by ignoring or fighting physical laws, but by hitching them up to human purposes. The social anarchy which now exists can be overcome only by a recognition of social laws, and by using them for human well-being. Now-a-days when a physical law is discovered, no one starts out to deny its existence or to fight against it, neither on theological nor on any other grounds. That day has passed. Scientists now explain the laws they find and show how to use them. It is not different in the social world. Sociology will undoubtedly be the most important study of the coming generation; it is the next great science. It comes at this time from the very womb of necessity. The advance in civilization made possible by other sciences had brought the world to that point where a solution of our social problems has become imperative.

Science applied to production, while solving the great problems of providing for the physical needs of humanity, has actually created other problems of no less importance, and it now remains to solve these. The benefits to the people which are possible from the advances made in the productive process are largely nullified by the inability to reorganize society upon a basis corresponding to the great industrial changes that have taken place. The supreme task of the twentieth century will be to find out how to make the many improvements of our scientific age yield happiness to all, instead of profit to a few, and the completion of this task is due now at any time. Ways of improvement must be found. Society cannot go on indefinitely as it now is, and indeed it will not do so, for the urge of economic laws continues to effect changes in the face of even the greatest opposition. By the power of natural forces in continual operation, society is being gradually reformed. The process is necessarily slow, but it is being retarded mainly by the reactionaries in power. While the operation of natural law in society cannot be ultimately frustrated, yet it may be hindered, on the one hand by mistaken opposition, or on the other helped by intelligent acquiescence. Things would be very different if in Canada, for instance, people understood the economic laws that are at work, and if the nation were organized in conscious co-operation with these laws, instead of blindly running in the very face of them.

DEMOCRACY AND THE GROUP

Self-preservation is the oldest, as it is still the most powerful law in human affairs. We may elevate idealism to the highest pedestal of human aspiration, and paint self-sacrifice as the crown of all moral achievement, but closer to life's center than these are the vital cords that hold humanity to its purposes. There is much too great a gap between our ideals and life's realities —such a gap, indeed, as to have completely severed the connection between the two, leaving ideals mockers of the soul rather than aids to achievement. Not that our ideals are too high, but rather that they are not natural, "Like sweet bells jangling out of tune." But the tragedy does not consist in the gap between ideals and the sordid realities of common life, the tragedy is that the "gap" is accepted as a matter of course. The man who affirms his belief in brotherhood, who would scorn to be called selfish, and who would consider it an offence to be suspected of unfair dealing, will amass a fortune without scruple. The business life of such a man is governed by the law of self-preservation. In obedience to it, he enters into competition for survival as well with his abstract brother as with his personal friend, while his cherished dreams of brotherhood vanish like a morning fog in the rising sun. The spirit of brotherhood does not live in the atmosphere of competition. There is, however, a higher social law urging itself upon society—that of co-operation, under which brotherhood will be possible. The law of co-operation has not been welcomed by humanity. It has been accepted to the extent that it has, only when self-preservation was seen to be impossible without it; it will be welcomed wholeheartedly only when it is seen that the self-preservation of the individual as well as of the whole are best secured by mutual aid.

As society develops, competition is becoming more and more impossible. Individuals, by the pressure of conditions, are driven into groups for common protection, and nations that at one time stood alone in competition with the world, are forced into alliances for protection against other alliances. The workman who used to compete for a job with his fellow now joins with him that together they may be the better able to look after the interests of both; the farmer, at one time the greatest example of an individualist, competing with his neighbor for land and markets, now makes common cause with him.

Strange as it may seem, competition itself is the father of co-operation, for competition when carried to a certain point becomes so destructive as to leave co-operation the only alternative to annihilation. Self-preservation, then, is the law which forced into existence the various co-operative units such as the Manufacturers' Association, the Trades Unions, and the United Farmers.

There is good reason to believe that man began his struggle on the animal plane. The sum of his life was the attainment of his physical wants. Self-preservation was the law which led primitive man into conflict with his fellows. Following on the heels of self-preservation was the law of parsimony—the obtaining of the greatest amount of returns for the least amount of effort, or the greatest pleasure for the least expense of pain. Competition was found to be the natural method of acting in obedience to these laws, and man adopted it. In the struggle between man and man which ensued, there was no place for the weak; those who survived were approximately of equal strength and cunning. Thus their struggles were evenly matched, and the natural justice resulting gave to each a share of the object of the struggle. By and by dawned reason. A new directive agent took charge of man's destiny. It looked down upon his struggle and suggested co-operation. The result was the tribe. By co-operating, the individuals who composed the tribe obtained at least as great a measure of justice by mutual arrangement as they obtained by the fighting of the earlier stage, and at the same time saved the energy that would have been expended in the struggle. Fellowship was promoted besides—which was so much to the good. Self-preservation then passed from the individual to the tribe. Competition thereafter took place only between one tribe and another. Those in turn continued to fight until collective reason taught them that co-operation would give them without the struggle all that they were competing to attain. Tribes then became a people, and the people became a nation.

In every case competition led to co-operation on a higher plane, competition being given up only when the existence of the individual, or the tribe, or the nation, was threatened by its retention. Then, nation entered into competitive struggle with nation. The objects of international strife were territory, trade, and commerce.

DEMOCRACY AND THE GROUP

Each nation fought for its own existence until among the smaller ones alliances became necessary in order to combat the larger and stronger. Thus alliances, or co-operation among nations for mutual benefit, have brought the world to that point where it is practically divided into two great armed camps. But this cannot last. The destructiveness of modern warfare is such that even the victor loses. Says a French paper, "We are free to weep. We are the victims of victory." The Great War demonstrates the impossibility of continuing the international struggle, as its continuance can only mean the eventual destruction of the race. Co-operation is the alternative. The League of Nations is the birth of the idea in its national aspect. We are approaching Tennyson's "parliament of man, the federation of the world." But it will come only when it is seen that it is necessary to self-preservation.

The high state of co-operation arrived at in the formation of the nation is based on the "group sense of safety." So far, people in a nation have only co-operated for self-defence against other nations. Individualism, until recently, has been supreme in our national economic life. But the end of individualism was hastened by the coming of the industrial revolution. When machinery was applied to industry, those who had control of the machinery entered into competition with each other for trade. To gain trade they had to sell cheaply, and to sell cheaply they had to exploit labor. In the exploitation of labor which followed, all suffered—men, women, and children. From that conscription there was no exemption. Wages were forced below the proper standard of living. When that happened the individual worker began to realize that as an individual competing with his fellows for work he was helpless. The workers were forced, therefore, to organize. The trades union came with its weapons of strikes and sabotage, and compelled the employer to pay a wage more adequate to purchase the necessities of life.

But what was the effect of this? It meant that the manufacturers could no longer compete with each other without mutual destruction. The Canadian manufacturers will serve as our illustration. Individualism was in their blood. They did not want to co-operate. But the law of self-preservation drove them to it, and the

Canadian Manufacturers' Association was formed. It is said that when the Canadian manufacturers met for the first time it was necessary to shut them up in separate rooms, so diverse were their opinions, and so keen was their competitive spirit. A messenger went from one room to the other exchanging their views, and working out a basis of organization, which basis was the common interest of self-protection. By their association the manufacturers' position was assured. They secured influence with governments, and were able to enter into successful competition with labor.

To offset the higher wages enforced by organized labor, the manufacturers obtained tariff privileges, and in addition added the extra wages to the price of the manufactured commodities. By their organization the industrial workers were able to maintain their position, but the burden of supporting the manufacturers' privileges was passed on to the unorganized workers. The farmer being the last in the line, it was passed on to him. The Canadian farmer became the dromedary of the nation. He had to pay what was asked, and take what was offered. He stood as an individual against highly organ-

145

ized economic groups. The inevitable happened. The farmer in turn organized. Everywhere failure was predicted for him. It was said, "They will never stick together." That can be said no longer. The cement or economic class interest which is self-preservation, that held the manufacturers and the labor unions, holds the farmers. As an economic group, forced to organize by necessity, the farmers now constitute the greatest and most important democratic unit in the nation.

I have traced the links in the chain of integration forged by the laws of social progress. The chain stretches from the individual savage to the federation of the world, and from the individual worker to highly organized economic groups. I have done this in the effort to show the inevitability of the farmers' movement, as well as to show that the same laws that have governed all previous development, are at work, and will eventually force us into a higher co-operation. Organized economic classes are now in competition in Canada, as in all other countries, for the lion's share of what has been jointly produced. As a result class war rages, not only in Canada, but in every civilized country in the world. That class war will go on until the collective mind discovers salvation in co-operation.

It is the economic question which goes to the very heart of our national problems. These problems must be solved, and they cannot be solved by competition; the groups which make competition cannot be destroyed; if they could be abolished it would mean turning back the wheels of progress. These groups must learn to co-operate between themselves in the same manner as individuals did in forming their several groups. This is what the laws of social progress say, and this is why we have a United Farmers' movement. But the farmers alone, of the economic groups in Canada, have discovered the higher law of co-operation. While other groups exist by co-operation, they do not see that co-operation must be applied between competing groups. Capital, highly organized, is engaged in a fight to the death with organized labor. The farmers come on the scene, just as the others came, but with a new discovery, namely, that farmers, laborers, manufacturers, and all other groups must co-operate to make a commonwealth of human happiness. Co-operation is the gospel of the United Farmers and their leaders are the apostles of it. Natural law is on their side, and co-operation will win. Competition cannot go much further without endangering the lives of the competing classes. Co-operation will ultimately be forced into existence between the competing groups, but if its mission could be realized and consciously striven after by all groups, as well as by the farmers, Canada might be saved a great deal of unnecessary suffering.

§2

Beginnings. Is group organization undemocratic? Those who oppose it say it is. I must therefore ask them the question, What is democracy? As I conceive democracy it would be as true to say that the foundation of a building was opposed to its walls, or that birth was opposed to maturity, as to say that group organization is opposed to democracy. Democracy is usually regarded as well understood and complete, seldom as the amorphous, still unfinished thing that it really is. Democracy is only beginning. In using the term beginning it must not be taken as opposed to the idea of continuation of progress from one age to another. In reality there is no

148

break; we continue from where we are with what we have; nevertheless we are, in a very real sense, at a "beginning" of many things, and, in particular, of practical democracy. A writer has said: "Man lives in the dawn forever. Life is beginning, and nothing else but beginning. It begins everlastingly." The humble beginning, on the part of groups of people, to think and act, and to accept responsibility for the conduct of their common life constitutes what may be called the birth of democracy.

There is much said and probably more written about democracy, but the real thing is constantly obscured by clouds of ink and words. Democracy is a very popular term—chiefly because nobody knows what is meant by it. In the name of democracy the politician seeks votes; the profiteer maintains his privilege of private ownership; jingoists call together armies to fight for it, and profit by the transaction. The disinherited, jobless worker holds democracy as a last hope, while judges and policemen for the sake and in the name of democracy imprison for preaching democracy, men who fought for democracy. Altogether it is a funny word; whatever it really means, it has been for a long time an "incomprehensible inscrutability." Not every one who says, "Lord, Lord!" is permitted to enter the Kingdom; neither is he the greatest democrat who has the term oftenest on his tongue.

The most popular, and most persistent, idea of democracy is related to the mob, or mass. That for which the greatest number of ballots have been cast is supposed to be the most democratic. Mob philosophy is the revolt against individualism. Time was when the individual could, and did, live unto himself. He was his own producer, his own distributor, his own master, and his own defence. To preserve himself was the whole aim of being. If preservation could not be attained by self there was no other way to attain it. The individual was and is the first and lowest unit in a society. When a large number of these units were thrown together in the evolutionary process, they were not thereby created a democracy. Not yet organized, they were little better than a mob, though organization was growing apace, and presently the herd emerged. The strongest or the most cunning of the herd became the ruler. His office was acknowledged because he sought to safeguard the rights of the individual, just as if there had occurred nothing to infringe upon those rights. But something had happened. People had been thrown together; and they had to learn now to live together. As tribes developed into nations the rulers gradually, while remaining of the people, drew apart from them, and were elevated above them. It was no longer necessary to be wiser, stronger, or more cunning in order to rule. It was necessary only to belong to the ruling class, or caste. Superstition by this time had built a wall of divine right around the throne, and the existing order was accepted as a matter of course. At the same time, the individual lost himself in the mob. There was but one individual left—the one at the top—and for him the rest existed. Societies of this type persisted for a long time. Then followed the revolt of the mob. The individual having been lost, there was nothing but the mob left, and so mob rule, or what is commonly called democracy, emerged. The mob still required rulers, of course—and so they elected them. The principal difference between the first and second cases was that in the first, the ruler ruled without votes, and by his own strength or cunning; while in the second the people voted for and chose their ruler, whose rule, thereafter, reposed on popular, or "mob" consent. It is now easy to see how necessary it was for the ruler, or those who worked in his behalf, to retain this popular consent, and why it has been held up till quite recently.

We are now, however, about to emerge from a mob-created government to the intelligent self-direction of an organized people. At the same time, it is of no use to blind ourselves to the fact that the mob is still most in evidence. A mob is a mob whether it is engaged in a lynching operation, or in throwing little pieces of paper into a ballot box. A mob might be defined as a number of people acting on an idea which does not belong to them; whereas a number of people acting on an idea, which, by a synthetic process involving a compounding of the different ideas of all the individuals concerned, is theirs, would be a democracy. A mob is incapable of thinking for itself, no matter how wise or clever the individuals composing it may be. Being incapable of creative thinking, and yet susceptible to ideas, an unorganized people will follow, in the one case, like sheep after a shepherd, and in another, will give chase like the wolf pack after its prey. There is no blame attached to the mob for acting in this way; if it acted in any other way it would not be a mob. If a mob is democracy then organized groups are essentially undemocratic. Few, however, will be found to entertain this view.

Organization of groups on the basis of common interest is gradually reducing the mob influence, although the latter still unfortunately predominates in most countries. Take the election in Great Britain immediately after the great war in 1918. There were more people who voted to hang the Kaiser than to reconstruct the economic life of the country. Organized labor, having learned to think in groups, did not follow the popular cry, but the unorganized masses did. We see similar effects in Canada. Although the people are supposed to govern, they never know what an election is going to be about until the campaign is on, and some mob psychologist announces the issue. Then follows a test of the hypnotic powers of the two parties, and the largest number of ballots is supposed to represent public opinion. In reality all that has happened is that we have learned which of the two parties had the greater influence on the mob. That mob susceptibility is a dangerous thing to have in a stable society is shown by the quick action of the authorities in arresting agitators. Politicians know what can be done by the hysterical appeals of agitators to a mass. They have won many elections in this way themselves, and know that a Labor agitator may meet with the same success if allowed, unhampered, to propagate *his* idea; so the agitator is arrested and jailed. It is just as dangerous to society when the people follow the jingoism of politicians during an election. But jingoes are not agitators for change—they are agitators for no change, a worse thing still, since it can end only in a cataclysmic upheaval and bloody revolution. If there were any cure in arrests, it were high time for the dishonest politicians of our time to be "run in" and called to account. But the remedy lies not in repression, it lies rather in education. The people must learn to think for themselves, not as individuals, but as groups. We seem to have been deluded into thinking that an opinion is a public one because the majority of the people have accepted it, whereas a public opinion must be an opinion created *by* the public, just as an individual opinion has been developed by an individual. The first thing to do, then, is to develop a real democratic thought. But this cannot be done by a mob. It can only be done by groups; and groups must be organized before they can think, and before they can be organized there must be a common interest to bring them together.

Democracy is in the becoming. It may be represented as a child. In the human infant are all the potentialities of achievement—as yet but dimly seen, and incoherent. The babe is physically helpless, unconscious, and dumb. But it is urged by natural laws, and in consequence asserts itself, and must continue asserting itself. The first effort to walk is apparently nothing more than an ineffective and meaningless kicking of the legs. But this kicking is neither meaningless nor ineffective; it is the beginning of greater things. The first attempt at expression is a cry, inarticulate except that it points to some pain that needs relief. These little means are not the end, they are manifestations in the child of an unfolding which will continue, perhaps, until all known human achievements are comprehended and new achievements added to those which are old.

Democracy must enter upon its career as a little child, and under the push of social laws must learn to achieve. The lowest possible democratic unit is the group. The birth of a group is the birth of democracy. That group, like the child, must learn to move as a unit, must become conscious of itself, and must learn to talk and express itself. When the group learns to speak it will not be the voice of an individual, it will be the voice of democracy. The opinion expressed by a group will not be the opinion of an individual, but a true group opinion. As the group advances in its thinking powers, it will become conscious of itself in relation to other groups, and will find its fuller life in a group of groups; and from that group of groups will come the consciousness and expression of a whole people, or, in other words, a democracy.

Democracy must now be defined as it is. It is well, at times, to give wings to fancy, and picture democracy in the ultimate, the ideal. But sooner or later we find our feet in the mud of reality. What is that reality? Democracy, *as it is,* may be defined to-day as a general utterance. I use utterance as expressive of thought, word, or deed. Utterance may be considered as development, as under-development is equivalent to incoherence. From this point of view democracy complete would be the common, united, and general utterance of the people as a whole, as distinguished from autocracy, the utterance of an individual or dominating class. But democracy is not completely developed. I have just spoken of it as a child newly born. And even as a child finds utterance by single words at the beginning, and later in the acquiring of a language forms sentences, so must the people find utterance gradually, until they can express themselves intelligently. A single word does not constitute a language, but languages, for all that, are composed of words. The first word or utterance of the child democracy is "group." No one claims that this word is all that democracy will ever be able to say. There are those who fear this word. They think it is a word that a child should not use. To-morrow the child will know other words such as cohesion, concentration, solidarity, united action, and co-operation.

In other words, the group is not the end of democracy, it is the beginning; it is democracy in its infancy in its first stages of development. The urge or principle which forms the group does not end when the group is formed, it continues to work until all groups are harmonized. But just as the individual does not lose his existence as an entity when he co-operates with other individuals to make a group, neither will the group lose its entity when it co-operates with other groups. Or, to return to my illustration of the child learning to speak, when it learns a new word, it does not forget the first word that it learned, but uses all its words as a means of expressing itself. When the complete democracy, which is the fullest utterance of the people, arrives, it will be composed of the group units that have helped to make it.

There are people who want to hurry progress. They want to leap from individualism to democracy at a jump. These people do no harm. Nature will not increase her speed for them, nor will she miss a step to please their fancy. Such people but reveal their childish opinions respecting life. The child will plant a seed in the evening, and be disappointed and discouraged because he cannot gather beans in the morning. It takes time to grow beans. It takes time to develop a democracy. Group organization is the first democratic unit. The impatient, unscientific mind may rave, but the laws of progress silently and slowly push on. They refuse to leap. They say that "co-operation must first be learned in the group." Democracy must pass through the group stage, just as the child must pass through adolescence to maturity. The group idea of the farmers does not claim for itself finality. It is only a step in the process, but a necessary step. Unless it is taken, the more developed democracy cannot come.

Democracy to-day is to be regarded as a united, collective, and general utterance, distinguished from partial or particular utterance. The body politic ought to have as united and homogeneous an organization as the body corporeal. The development of the various parts of each ought to synchronize and concur.

Having decided that groups are necessary to democracy—where are we to find them? If democracy must pass through group stages to the fullest development, there is no use talking about democracy until the child democracy— the group—is born. But this group cannot be produced artificially. Like the child it must be born naturally; a political incubator cannot produce it. The democratic progeny of the political incubator are short-lived monstrosities. The incubator proceeds on the theory that grouping people together on the basis of an idea is the way to do the trick. The idea is called a political platform. It is made by interested individuals. As people must either be for or against such a platform they naturally divide into two parties and engage in fighting each other. I deal in another section with the "idea" as a basis for group organization, and so will say here simply that the idea or ideas incorporated in a party platform, whether followed by approximately half the people of a country or any other proportion, are not the people's ideas. The people have nothing to do with these ideas; for the time being they follow them; that is all. They are not expressing themselves as a natural group. There comes an election, and it is lost or won, but when the election is over, there is no organization left. The people have only been voting together as individuals, they have not been thinking and acting together as a unit, and, consequently, there is no democracy. Voting for a platform, or an "idea" created by some individual, will never develop democratic responsibility. When a platform has not been adhered to by a government, or when the ideas incorporated in it turn out to be false, what happens? Those who voted for it, properly blame those who thought out the platform, and who were allowed to translate it into practical legislation. No! There can never be a democracy as long as the people are justified in blaming certain individuals; as soon as we have a measure of democracy it will mean that the people accept responsibility for their thoughts and acts, and as they cannot think nor act until they are organized into democratic units, the units must first exist. And as these units or groups canot be created artificially, the only thing to do is to rely on the natural laws which operate in the creation of these units.

§3

Groups Based on Ideas. Those who oppose the group idea as advocated and adhered to by the United Farmers, particularly of Alberta, argue that an "idea" should be the common basis for the forming of a group; that, otherwise, people in agreement with the group would be prohibited from joining it, especially if the group rested on an economic basis; and

161

11

further, that if ideas be substituted for economic laws that the group will get away from that selfishness which is characteristic of Trades Unions and Manufacturers' Associations. This kind of talk sounds well to the gallery at a political meeting, but it has no basis in fact, and it completely overlooks the laws of human relations. But let us examine these arguments and decide as to their impracticability.

If people can be united by an idea, it follows that they may also be divided by an idea. The only sure way of maintaining unity in that case would be to find people who all thought the same thing, but every schoolboy knows that to find people who think alike is impossible. It may be doubted if any two people think alike, or even approximately alike, on any one thing, not to speak of the many things involved in the life of a nation. What stability, therefore, could be expected from an organization based upon an idea? It is true, of course, that a mass may grab an idea and act upon it during an election, but an organization cannot be built on that, because the common idea is only of momentary duration; the people who, for election purposes, were brought together by some idea are driven poles apart by disagreements on other ideas as soon as the election is over. Moreover, the ideas that intrigue the mass are usually surface ideas only; they represent not even average thoughts, but *in reality the lowest thought,* for what everybody knows about is of necessity the most general and most commonplace. The thought which captivates the mass is like the froth on the beer, sparkling and attractive, but froth withal. The deeper and more solid issues are never so much as hinted at, and when by chance a real economic point is mooted it divides the people, inasmuch as the economic outlook depends a good deal upon who is looking out, and from where he is looking. The wage earner, the employer, the business man, the public, the farmer, and the manufacturer, do not all see the same thing when they look at our economic life. True they are all looking at the same thing, but from vastly different angles. Where the farmer sees higher prices for wheat, the railways and the banks and wheat dealers see less profit, the public a higher price for bread, and the worker diminished purchasing power. Inasmuch, then, as ideas vary with the individuals or classes possessing them, to organize a people on the basis of an idea is impracticable. And it is well for progress that this is so. Could people be organized permanently on the basis of a common idea, thought would perish. If we want to make a mental cemetery out of Canada, this would be a good way to do it. But if our nation is to be a veritable factory of ideas people of many different thoughts must be able to unite. Then, by the interplay of different minds, a creative social thought becomes possible, and every individual becomes a part creator.

But economic interests are always stronger and more determining in an organization than ideas. There are in every country organizations which may be said to be based on ideas, but the part they play in real life is almost nothing. It is a common thing to find in the constitutions of such organizations that matters of religion and politics are barred, which, of course, is bound to mean that the organization is sterile, and barren of effect. Suppose we could bring a manufacturer, a farmer, and a laborer, into one fraternal society. The idea which brings them together is brotherly love, we shall say. But a strike comes on; the workman fights the manufacturer, and the manufacturer fights the workman, while the farmer fights both. The brotherly love idea vanishes. They may meet in their organization while the industrial fight is going on, but the meeting would be a meaningless farce. It is because economic interests always divide people that so many societies bar economic questions and political matters. But is it wise to ignore a law which despite all fraternal oaths—oaths, constitutions, and treaties—operates against fraternalism? Why not face these facts of life and grapple with them, as the United Farmers are doing? As long as the problems are ignored, or barred from discussion, people may be united, but it will be upon such unreal grounds that the problems they exist, presumably, to solve, are forever impossible of solution, as their different interests still divide them. Better, by far, is it to have an organization which exists principally to face and discuss the issues that divide people. Otherwise the unity which people seek by ignoring divisions, since it is entirely artificial, is liable to split up at any moment. If it be that people never do think alike, that if they did it would be detrimental to progress, and if it be that economic needs are so much stronger to divide than ideas are to unite, the impracticabil-

ity of organizing a people on an idea basis so as
to act as a unit in political affairs will be evident. The line of least resistance is the one to
follow, not the line of greatest; and no idea can
bring together where interest creates a division.
Possibly the line of least resistance *should* be
anywhere but where it is, but unfortunately—it
isn't.

Pursuing this further, it will be seen that those
objecting to the class, or group, idea of organization, on the ground that the "idea," and not
the class, should be the cause of people coming
together, derive their thought from autocratic
sources. If people are to be organized on an
"idea," who is to furnish the "idea"? If the
greatest thinkers were allowed to provide the
idea the results might not be so disastrous. But
when a great thinker advances an idea, what
happens? He is either ignored, imprisoned, or
crucified. The masses do not understand him,
and therefore, cannot follow him. It is only a
surface idea that will be appreciated by a majority, and that idea is made "for" people, and
surely if people are going to be organized on an
idea someone must find the idea. This is the
most objectionable phase of the question. Peo-

ple must not be thought for any longer, they must do their own thinking; and must themselves create social thought. Collective thinking is the greatest achievement of the United Farmers' movement. Its policies and ideals have been developed from the thoughts of its members; it is a movement without a Kaiser or dictator. To abandon this most democratic position, attained by much struggle, would be to rob the organization of one of its most distinctive features, and reduce it to a commonplace level where it could not justify its existence.

The farmers' platform is the result of creative, collective thinking. Unlike ordinary political parties, the farmers do not have to shape their minds to a previously made platform, it is necessary only for them to shape their platform according to their collective mind. Just here is to be found the most significant difference between the platform of the agrarian movement, and that of the political parties. The platform of the parties is made by interested leaders; it is the first thing to appear, then follows the organization composed of people who can swallow the platform without mental and moral indigestion.

The farmers went about their political activities in a much more sane and natural way. They knew that if anyone made a platform for farmers it would not be a farmers' platform, they knew that it was impossible to know what the farmers wanted until they were organized, and until they had given expression to their own thoughts. Accordingly, organization took place first; the platform followed after. Questions of national interest from the farmers' viewpoint were first discussed in the locals. Each member brought to the discussion the best contribution of which he was capable. When the various thoughts of the members had been harmonized and embodied in a resolution, that resolution was forwarded to the Canadian Council of Agriculture. This was not done by one local, but by all. Then the Canadian Council of Agriculture, which is composed of elected representatives, made a selection of the issues decided upon by the various locals, compiled them into a platform, and sent the platform back to the annual provincial conventions, there to be ratified or rejected. The farmers' platform is therefore a democratic production. There has never been anything like it before in the history of Canada. It is the first real democratic utterance of political significance to be heard in Dominion politics; it is a product of creative thinking, brought about by the interpenetration of the thoughts of individual members, and synthetised into a set of political principles capable of standing any test to which they may be subjected. Being the thoughts of the farmers themselves, each member accepts the responsibility implied, and a strange new feeling of power and freedom inspires each farmer to work with enthusiasm for the success of his own political enterprise.

Thought is not the first thing in the natural order of things. The mind is the flower of personality, it is the last thing to develop. A child does not think before it is born, neither does an organization think before it is organized. Thought, then, cannot be the *basis* of an organization that is democratically formed; thought is the highest thing and comes last. A common interest and not a common thought is the true basis of a natural group. That interest may be sentimental, it may be artistic or scientific, or it may be economic. When these, or other, interests draw people together into a group their thoughts are not tampered with; each member may think differently from the rest on a thousand things. The greater the diversity of thought, in fact, the greater the intellectual advancement of the group. But the strongest bond is the interest that brought them together, and the strongest of all interests is the economic one. This interest has stood the test of history; it is operating to-day with its same compelling power, unobtrusively shaping the destiny of nations. Repudiate it at your peril; call it selfishness, or any other name you wish, what will that profit you? The apple falls just the same, call gravity what you will. Face the facts. Groups do exist in Canada, as in every other country, and they exist as the outcome of industrial interests, and in all the land there are no more powerful or influential organizations to be found. The manufacturers' association is an economic group, and one of the smallest in numbers, yet its power in Canadian politics is great. It may be questioned if our religious and educational institutions have made as great an impression on public life as has the manufacturers' association and its plutocratic alliance. By controlling the government the ruling class controls both organized religion and education, and a knowledge of this fact sufficiently answers the question. The farmers' organization is an industrial group, brought together by a common industrial interest, and it is about to challenge the privilege of the manufacturers' association to run the affairs of the nation. Not that the farmers seek to dominate. They do not. Nor do they deny the manufacturers, or other groups, their proper share in the control of national affairs. This they could not do if they would; but what *is* sought is that on account of the industrial necessities of the agriculturalists, adequate representation in the legislative bodies of the country be given to the farmers' organization no less than to the organizations of the other interests.

If the class basis is ignored the strength of the movement is dissipated. People who are not farmers cannot appreciate the farmers' interests, and if they were allowed to control the farmers' organization it would cease to be a farmers' movement, and would degenerate into a political party of the old school, dividing one farmer against another on an "idea" which very likely would not have very much to do with anything of any value. A political party organization is only in politics once in four years. Its function is to get votes. The farmers' organization rests upon the interests of the industry, which are permanent, and they are in politics all the time, continuously studying the issues, and seeking to direct affairs in accordance with their own thought. In other words, party politics is an autocratic machine for electing rulers, while the farmers' movement is democratic and aims at self-government.

It may be pointed out that economic class interest is in itself an idea. To the extent that the class interest must pass through the consciousness of the individual, it is of the nature of an idea, but the critics of the United Farmers distinguish between the economic group consciousness and an ordinary political idea, or platform. In this they are right. The difference is fundamental. When the United Farmers refuse to be organized on what their critics call "ideas" it does not mean that they disparage ideas. On the contrary, it means that they think ideas so important that they cannot afford to permit anyone to make their ideas for them. Just as the philosophy of an individual is a synthesis of all the ideas and experiences which have come to that individual during life, so a social philosophy must be a synthesis of all the thoughts of a number of individuals. The United Farmers are making their group a social entity capable of creative thought, and of self-direction, and as such it will be one of the greatest, if not the greatest, contribution to democratic progress in a century.

§4

Group Politics. Why enter politics as a group? An answer must be found to this question. Sincere as well as insincere people are asking it. The United Farmers are taking political action as an economic group. The masses whose political views belong to the party system do not understand group politics. In this there would seem to be an element of sincerity. They conceive of politics as belonging to all the people, and as being separate from industrial interests. They are afraid that group politics may lead to dissension, to class domination, and perhaps to political chaos. For these reasons, it is incumbent upon the advocates of group politics to prove conclusively that these fears are without foundation. What has already been said on the necessity of groups to collective thinking, and their natural development in the evolutionary process, should make apparent the advantages of preserving these group units in politics. But for greater clarity I will further amplify and explain.

To begin with, farmers are taking group political action because they are convinced that party politics is corrupt and inefficient. This being the case, there is for them no alternative. In seeking to substitute some other method for partyism, the farmers have the support of the masses, but many who see the corruption and inefficiency of partyism are not in favor of groups. These people think that they can get rid of partyism by making a new party. The farmers think that to get rid of partyism you must get rid of the party idea altogether. As was shown earlier in the book, partyism is not only becoming morally degenerate, but since it fails to give expression to the expert opinion of economic groups, representative of new conditions, it is thoroughly obsolete as well. That being so, these economic groups must find political expression or the country will have to take the consequences in direct action. We have seen that collective opinion must be developed if democracy is to be a success; and that group organization is the basis for forming collective opinion. But what shall we do with this collective opinion? It is useless to form collective opinion if there is no way of expressing it. Group politics, therefore, is necessary for the expression of collective opinion, if it cannot be expressed through party politics. The farmers have been voting for party candidates ever since Confederation, but they have never had representation; their industry has been ignored by legislators, and the voice of their opinions has been drowned in the party cry. Their political schooling has been long and severe. Shall they forget the lesson so hardly learned? Would you have them perpetuate, by their own will and design, the very injustice against which they have organized? Until recently there have been practically no farmers in our legislative assemblies: professional and business interests have controlled our governments. It is the party system which has permitted them to do so. The farmers know this, and have decided to try some other way.

That semblance of unity which constitutes the appeal of the parties is at once its virtue and its most obvious weakness, its virtue in that it attracts the mass by its appearing to embrace all, its weakness in that it is merely a semblance after all. It pretends to be out in the interests of all the people. This is its attractiveness. No one wishes to support any section or group having designs for domination. And even though our modern governments have always failed to legislate for all, inasmuch as they have ruled by and for the moneyed interests, their appeal is always made on the basis of the general well-being. This appeals to the imagination. It has the ring of democracy, but the ring only. If the opposers of group politics could see that there is another way, and a better one, of reaching the common good, which partyism ever pretends but never practises, there should be no difficulty in winning them to the group philosophy.

I have said that the pretence of the parties to stand for all people is their greatest weakness. The reason for this must be obvious. In these days of complicated social problems, that party or individual is indeed bold, who assumes the ability to represent all classes and all opinions. And yet this is precisely what a party, or party leader, does. A lawyer, without even giving the slightest evidence of a knowledge of the impossibility of his task, will stand up before an audience and tell them that he is able to make laws to suit all of them. To do so, he must represent the agrarians, including wheat growers, horticultural workers, sheep raisers, cattle raisers, fruit growers, lumber men, etc., he must also make laws to meet the requirements of industrial workers, such as railway men, miners, builders, textile workers, workers in manufacturing establishments of all kinds; he must make laws dealing with the price of wheat, the price of implements necessary for farming, laws dealing with the price of transportation, and of all the products of a nation's industry; he must make laws regulating work and wages, hours of work, sanitary conditions, workmen's compensation, etc. In addition, he must make laws to suit bankers, manufacturers, landlords, railroad magnates, and professional people of all classes; and most important of all, he must submit absolutely to the dictates of the party caucus. Where is there such a man? Let us grant, for the sake of argument, that our hypothetical lawyer is free to make laws for all these people, free in so far as the influence of certain interests is concerned (which he would not be), the question still re-

mains, Has he the ability? He certainly has
not. His lack of knowledge makes it impossible. No one man to-day can know sufficiently
the outlook of all industrial classes and their several interests to be able to make laws that will
give justice to them all. In a simpler society, it
was more nearly possible to do so, as I have already indicated, but at no time since.

Perhaps, it might be as well for the sake of
clearness to emphasize here the significance to
politics of our industrial age. Let us enter a
workshop in England a hundred years ago. It
is a joiners' shop. There are very few workers
employed, but as many as there are have all
served long apprenticeships to their trade, and
each knows it thoroughly. For instance, each
joiner knows how to make a door. He takes it
from the rough lumber, dresses it, cuts it to the
proper size, draws it in, mortices it, panels, pegs,
and even paints it. He knows all about the making of a door; so do all his brother joiners. If
you were to take a vote on any question pertaining to the making of a door, you could depend
upon getting an intelligent answer. But let us
enter a factory of the present day, and note what
we find. Machinery has destroyed the art of

door-making. The grandchildren, or the great-grandchildren, of those men we saw in the factory a hundred years ago, are also engaged in making doors; but it takes them all to make one. Alone, none of them could make it. Each has a definite place in which to stand, and a definite piece of machinery to operate. In the factory, they never even see a door—a complete door, that is—they see it only in parts. If you were to take a vote in that factory on some question relating to a door, you might find as many different opinions on that question as a door has different parts. But if you made no provision for the registering of these definite opinions, using the old ballot that you used in the previous factory, it would be impossible to get to know the different opinions which these men had about making doors. Or again, if you found a question relating to a door, which would be understood by all these men, it could only be, at the present time, a question of the most simple and non-essential sort. This is a change that the introduction of the machine process had made in one craft only, and similar changes have been made in every other trade. The workers of the world have been divided into groups under its disintegrating and specializing rule. One group digs the coal, another digs the iron, one group smelts the iron with the coal, another manufactures it into commodities, yet another transports it, while still another group grows the food for all these groups together. While one group cannot get along without the others, yet they know little of each other's immediate needs. Miners do not understand the needs of store clerks, farmers do not understand those of wage workers, wage workers those of professional people, and so on. But the laws that govern the lives of all these people are made without consulting a single group concerned, by another group—a group apart—no member of which is in contact with any other group.

Just as in the case of the factory then, there are in a nation as many different interests and different ways of attending to these interests as there are groups. The old party system assumes that there are only two possible opinions, one for and one against its own program. But the question which could be understood by all would necessarily be, as I just now pointed out, a very simple and non-essential question indeed. For this reason the parties totally ignore economic questions in elections. They must. To be successful they must find an issue that is on the surface of things, that everybody knows about, and almost the only issue of which this is true is that spurious brand of patriotism that for so long has done yeoman service. So it comes about that our parliamentarians are frequently ignorant and incapable of the duties they assume. Philosophers and economists could hardly be expected to allow themselves to be elected on the ordinary party cry. Such would be an insult to their honesty and intelligence. For this and other reasons, the ablest, mentally and morally, are seldom found in Parliament.

The obtaining of a majority is the aim of party politics. Party majorities, however, make no provision for expressing, and have not themselves the means of expressing the special intelligence developed through specialization in industry. "The more the intelligence is trained and educated, the more all different groups are by training and education specialized, the lower is the grade of intelligence which they all together have in common."* Consequently, party governments invariably represent the lowest in-

---

*"Public Policy," Cooling, Page 8.

telligence of the nation. The intelligence of an industrial unit is infinitely higher, in matters pertaining to its own life, at least, than that which any individual may have respecting all the groups. The group ideas are stable, they are not subject to the whims of individuals, or the scare cries of demagogues. This is one reason why they are thought to be dangerous by those who, taking advantage of the popular consensus, which consensus is usually concerned with questions of relative unimportance, lay up for themselves the profits and privileges it should be their highest duty to conserve for the public good. In a majority vote on a popular and relatively unimportant issue, the witless may outvote the wise, but it too frequently happens that it is those who live by their wits who win. Now if, by group politics, the farmers can preserve their collective opinion, and find representation for it in the national assembly, not only will they have performed a service to themselves, but in breaking away from party politics and all it stands for, they will have done a service to civilization.

Once more then, the farmers do not seek domination. They seek representation. Simply that. They urge also, that all other groups seek representation. How, then, can the farmers be charged with a low selfishness, when they are advising all others to seek what they seek for themselves? And just as they hope to obtain what they are out for, they are not behindhand in hoping that other groups, also, will be equally successful. Every industrial group to-day knows that it cannot live by itself, or to itself. If one group were to secure political power and use that power to the detriment of any other group, it would ultimately kill itself. Farmers cannot live without coal miners, city dwellers without railroad workers, nor industrial workers without farmers. Each depends on all, and all depend on each. This social unity is not overlooked by group politics. And surely when the various groups are necessary to the lives of all, all ought to be represented in that parliament which deals with their common life, so that in bringing to the service of the nation the best knowledge from every group, they may be able, co-operatively, to arrive at the highest justice.

Society may be represented as an organism; the higher an organism develops, the more complex its parts become. The human organism has developed from a simple splotch of protoplasm. Included in that organism are many parts, hands, feet, stomach, heart, eyes, ears, and brains, etc. All have special functions to perform. No one would think of arguing that the development of these various organs meant anarchy, that the hands would carry off the lungs, or the feet walk off with the nerves; on the contrary, it is well-known that in the pursuit of the purpose of the intelligence, every organ becomes of service, acting in co-operation for the well-being of the organism. Society is like the human body. Once it was a social plasm, the simple form. As it evolved, it developed many parts and functions, in the performance of which groups of people act as units. It would be insane, if it were possible, to throw a man into a chemical solution that would reduce him into his original protoplasm for the sake of sameness and primitive unity. For surely the unity of parts acting in harmony is higher and more admirable than the original bit of jelly. But this is exactly what some people want to do with our groups. They are trying to throw the groups into a political solution which will reduce their distinctive solidified functional organization into the original party jellyfish; and they are doing this, if you please, in the name of unity.

It is not inconsistent with harmony to have different groups. Harmony, in fact, without their existence, is impossible. The song of a primitive people is simple and monotonous, because their emotions are simple; but as they rise in the evolutionary scale and acquire deeper and more complicated feelings, a corresponding change is found in their musical expression. Music then develops parts. But when the separate parts of music are sung together, they do not produce a medley of sounds, they produce harmony. And hundreds of instruments playing various parts together make a symphony. Similarly, the primitive party intelligence may be expressed as a simple monotone, and it is this simple monotone that party advocates still wish a highly developed people to chant. But, having risen in the scale of social evolution, the Canadian people has thoughts and aspirations which can no longer be expressed through the party machine. As groups, or parts, of our national life, the different classes must be brought together, and in their coming together we hope to have that economic harmony of which so many have dreamed, or if you like, we hope to achieve out of the present welter, a political symphony.

The antagonism to the group idea finds its source in the group philosophy of other movements that are considered revolutionary. Syndicalism is based on industrial groups. Its group formation is its virtue. But its teaching in respect of the state, which by its opponents is held to be objectionable and impractical, is not a necessary corollary of group organization. Syndicalism aims at the overthrow of the state; it seeks to invest each syndicate or group with full control of all that pertains to the life of the syndicate. There is no provision made for the unification of the syndicates so as to regulate the interlocking and common interests of all. On the contrary, syndicalism openly advocates the abolition of the state. Its logical outcome would be anarchy. The syndicalists, while creating members of one body, refuse to allow the bodies themselves to federate. In contrast to the syndicalists are the Bolsheviki with their soviets. It would appear that industries and professions form the basis of the soviet system. But here, again, we find a departure from the logic of the group idea. From the industrial basis the syndicalist works toward a stateless civilization, while the Bolshevik, from the same basis, arrives at a rigid state control. Every step which the soviet system takes from the industrial group leads farther away from the people toward autocracy until it culminates in a dictatorship. The industrial system centralized in this dictatorship becomes a bureaucracy which may in time become as intolerable and inefficient as private ownership under Czarism. The syndicalist theory and the soviet state both start from the same basis, and reach diametrically opposite results. Neither system has followed the natural co-operation which underlies the group organization. The Bolsheviki in following the teachings of Marx are in danger of reaching an industrial bureaucracy and a political dictatorship, while the syndicalists in adhering to the teachings of Bakunin are heading toward anarchy. The Guild socialists, also, advocate a group system which is, perhaps, the sanest and most practical of all European theories of social improvement. They strive to find a synthesis between the anarchy of Bakunin and the bureaucracy of Marx. The guild is to have democratic control of the industry, but according to guild socialism there must be also a central control or state for the supervision of all industries for the common good, and to prevent strife arising between one industry and another. But this central body, or parliament, is to be elected in a manner similar to that in vogue at the present time. This is the weak spot in guild socialism. The parliament should be the elected representatives of the various guilds, and thus preserve the opinions, and represent the interests, of each democratic unit in the state.

The industrial group system as taught by the United Farmers of Canada implies all the good points of the systems reviewed, and none of their weaknesses or errors. Indeed the Canadian farmers are evolving the most admirable political system on record. As an industrial organization the farmers' movement will direct and control its own affairs as an industry, allowing the same privilege to all other groups, but it insists that representatives of organized industries shall compose the parliament. The key to the political philosophy of the United Farmers is co-operation. The co-operation which brought individuals together in a group must be applied between the groups until the highest form of co-operation is reached, namely, a fully organized co-operative state.

According to this philosophy, economic and political questions are inseparable. The farmer will not entrust his politics to one party and his economics to another. Politics to him is but the direction of economic affairs, and in order that economic affairs may have the proper direction, farmers must personally help to direct them, and, accordingly, it is for this purpose that they seek representation in parliament as a group. And why not? Is there any good reason for going back to individualism in politics? The argument that it is well to organize industrial groups, but a mistake for these to take political action on account of their possible group selfishness, is unsound. If an industrial group is too selfish to be serviceable in politics, it will be selfish all through, so why admit the usefulness of its organization for any purpose whatever? When a farmer is raising wheat, he considers that he is performing work that has quite as much to do with the life of the nation as he would be if he were helping to make laws governing the price of wheat. The same argument which justifies the existence of the industrial organization will justify, if it is sound, political action on the part of such an organization. Inasmuch as the farming industry is affected by politics, the farmer must be in politics. He must follow his industry. If it goes to parliament, the farmer must go too. But as a law affecting agriculture does not influence farmers alone, but has an influence on other industries, it is necessary that representatives of other industries as well as farmers should have something to do with the making of law. Instead of having lawyers in parliament making laws under the delusion that the laws they make are good for everybody, we must have the laws made by representatives of the people who are affected by the laws, and who are to live under the laws.

Economic problems—and all these are economic problems—cannot be solved by parties; not because the parties do not *want* to solve them, but because they do not know *how*. Instead of trying to solve the problem party men ignore it. But to ignore the existence of the problem, or endeavor to suppress the symptoms of it, or turn a blind eye on its effects, is dangerous. This course inevitably leads to revolution, and unless we desire that outcome, it is a course that must be abandoned. The other course—that of group politics—would admit the existence of economic differences, but while admitting them, would, at the same time, face and solve them. Economic questions will be best and soonest solved by economic groups. Let labor, farmer, professional, and business representatives meet around one common table. Let them bring with them their differences and difficulties, and, in the spirit of co-operation, find a solution that will give most satisfaction to all. This course is reasonable, moral, and practicable. If the best intelligence of the various group organizations cannot find, in the principle of co-operation, a better than the present way of doing things, what hope is there? It is in the expectation of bringing about a truly co-operative commonwealth that the farmers are entering politics as a group.

Group politics is the only way in which it is possible to accept responsibility, and it were well if at this moment every group or organization in Canada were prepared to take the same step as that now being taken by the United Farmers. The farmers have organized, and have developed a group opinion as expressed in their platform. They are going to elect men in and by their groups, and are accepting the responsibility involved. This being the case, the farmers cannot afford to lose control of their own political movement. As one old farmer puts it, "Our political horse is high strung, and he has been standing in the stable so long that he is feeling his oats. We can't afford to allow a tenderfoot to draw the lines over the critter, or he will run away and smash the whole outfit." That expresses the situation precisely. Either the farmers must take group political action and thus control their own political thoughts and conduct, or incur the danger of a political runaway. It must be group representation and co-operation; or mass hysteria and party domination.

§5

Class Legislation. The Ontario election of October, 1919, which swept the Hearst government from its moorings, and left the farmers' group the strongest in the legislature, and the subsequent Dominion bye-elections that chose every farmer who offered himself, combined to affect profoundly the two historic parties, their lords, the financial interests, and their lackeys, the press. Nothing in the political history of Canada ever presented such a formidable challenge to partyism and privilege. The phenomenal success of the agrarian movement in Ontario, and the determination shown by the other provinces to follow Ontario's lead constituted a rude awakening to complacent politicians, hitherto secure in their assurance of power. Before the Ontario election the farmers' political ambitions were not considered seriously. It was thought, and not without reason, that when the old party war drums sounded the call to an election, the farmers would forget their allegiance to their own group and rush to the traditional stamping ground. This had been the case in other independent political adventures. But there was something which party men could not account for in the farmers' campaign. The solid front shown in the contest by the new forces revealed the strength of their organization. Their success wrote upon the walls of Canadian history the first real prophecy of the downfall of economic privilege and political corruption. Ontario was lost to privilege, but from every political watch-tower in the Dominion sounded the rallying call to arms. The conviction of its enemies is that the farmers' movement must be stopped, and with this stopping of it in view the Canadian press has worked overtime. It has attempted to discredit the United Farmers with the public, and to undermine the faith of the individual farmer in his own organization and ideals. Partyism, and all that stands behind it, are fighting for life. If the farmers' organization cannot be destroyed, the day of partyism is done. There is no mistaking the issue, and there is no misunderstanding the motive of the party press in concentrating its heavy artillery and gas upon the center of the agrarian movement. So far the attack has served only to weld the farmers together, and has demonstrated that a movement is not weakened by opposition from without. If the heart of the movement be true, and its members enlightened and loyal, outside antagonism will not avail to overthrow it, but will on the contrary solidify and establish it. Becoming aware of the futility of its efforts from without, the opposition is trying now to create dissension in the farmers' ranks, from within. The "Class Legislation" cry is being used for this purpose. The farmer is known to be an enemy of class legislation. If he can be made to believe that class organization is equivalent to class legislation, the work of the enemy will be complete. For the farmers would then invite the enemy to join the movement, so as to prove antagonism to class legislation. And when the farmers thus yield the direction of their organization to their enemies, they will cease to be a factor of any consequence. It is, therefore, of the utmost importance that the "class legislation" cry of the party press be thoroughly examined.

In trying to saddle the farmers with class legislation, the purpose of the party press is not to save Canada from such an unmitigated evil. For forty years the party press of Canada has defended class legislation. Labor men and socialists have persistently pointed out that the government of Canada, regardless of which party formed it, was dominated by plutocrats, and legislated for Big Interests. Throughout our history the press has been the bulwark of that system which lived and prospered by means of class legislation. That press is still in the service of the class that has made all the legislation on our statute books, but never, in all the years, has the press uttered one word of protest.

Content to pick the crumbs that fell from the privileged table, it has been mute while our natural resources were being plundered, and while individuals were securing, through legislation, monopolies of basic industries. Why this sudden outburst of indignation? Is this a deathbed repentance, or merely a trick of the fox to escape its would-be captors? Surely, since the time Sir John A. Macdonald introduced his national policy, there has been some opportunity to object to class legislation. That policy, however indispensable it may have been at the time, and regardless of what incidental good may have resulted from it, was a class policy. It was a class policy that concentrated wealth in the hands of a few, and placed our political and economic destiny at the will and mercy of the few who had the wealth. The policy inaugurated by Sir John A. Macdonald, sustained by Sir Wilfrid Laurier, and upheld by Sir Robert Borden, was a plutocratic class policy, if ever there was one. It was, and is, defended by the press. In its charge of class legislation against the farmers, then, where is the logic of the press attack, or on what moral grounds does it make its appeal? No, logic it has none—nor moral grounds either. It has audacity and nothing more.

The record of the Canadian press is such as to stamp its present attitude to the farmers' movement as wholly insincere and totally inadequate as well. To find these parties, that since Confederation have burdened the nation with the most hideous forms of class legislation, accusing of just such legislation the farmers who have organized—as the victims of class governments always must organize—in order to overthrow and put an end forever to class legislation, and to find these accusations upheld and multiplied by the party press, and the accusers white-washed and kalsomined to the point of being made to appear, and being foisted on the public, as the shining guardians of liberty and democracy in the act of resisting the insidious encroachments of inimical black legions—this, without question, is the most monstrous perversion of the truth imaginable—the very limit of preposterousness. To preach to the United Farmers on democracy and justice, as it is now doing, the party press has no warrant. Its chief purpose, of course, is to save the party system, and to maintain class legislation in the interests of those for whom the press exists. But to the farmers, as well as to most other people, knowing the history and function of the party press as they do, its present purpose is altogether too obvious to be taken seriously, even for a moment.

The history of Canada is the record of the rise, development, and supremacy of class rule. Class domination reached its peak in the Union Government, which was ostensibly formed to further our cause in war, but which in reality was nothing more than the co-operation of the plutocratic classes for the domination and exploitation of the dominion. Always between these classes there had been, prior to 1917, some measure of rivalry. This rivalry usually found expression in the political parties; certain elements supported the Liberals to serve them, while others looked to the Conservatives. So long as there was a degree of competition among the plutocratic classes, just so long was there an element of justice in their various party administrations, but with the emergence of the Union Government the plutocratic classes combined, and every semblance of democracy vanished from Canadian public life. The first outrage was the election act, by means of which the servants of plutocracy were elected. There probably never was an act upon the statute books of any English speaking country so manifestly "classy" in its origin and application, as the act by which the Union Government legislated itself into power. It was so disgraceful as to bring the blush of shame to every Canadian who felt any pride in the boasted freedom of his country. Whether the disfranchisement of Canadian citizens brought about by the act could be justified on patriotic grounds is open to question, but that many were deprived of the ballot who were loyal Canadians cannot be doubted, neither is their any question that many who were enfranchised by the act had no better qualification than many who were disfranchised. On the coming to power of the Union Government, parliament was virtually done away with, its place being taken by orders-in-council. Here was class legislation, the most flagrant and brazen ever perpetrated. Kaiserism made its abode in Ottawa,—where it still flourishes. The *iron heel* of censorship was placed on the *neck* of every protester. Literature in opposition to plutocratic class rule was banned, and the worst features of the inquisition were not too bad to be resurrected and brought to Canada to do service in the interest of a class tyranny of the most shameful kind. It is very doubtful if at any other time such abuses of liberty would have been tolerated. The loyalty of Canadians to the cause of the Allies enabled them to endure what ordinarily they would have resisted. All repression and persecution was carried out in the name of patriotism, and so once more one of the noblest impulses of the human heart was trampled upon. Open revolt or patient suffering were the only alternatives before the Canadian people, and in order not to prejudice the cause in Europe they chose the latter. But reaction was inevitable. It smouldered, under cover of patience and loyalty, until peace was declared, and then at every opportunity it flamed up. Every bye-election was hailed with joy because it brought the opportunity to give a well-merited rebuff to autocracy.

Judging from the present temper of the Canadian people, they have had about enough of class rule. Their determination is to abolish it. And in its abolition the farmers are destined to play an important part. The climax of class rule has come. The plutocrats, through their servant the Union Government, have undone themselves by their insatiable appetite. The working class, including the farmers, is living now far below the standard of life of 1914; the country is obliged to shoulder enormous debts unscrupulously incurred under the cover of the war; the profiteers have made a sum approximately equal to that of the swollen national debt; the cost of living still ascends, while the repeated issuance of bonds to raise the money with which to pay the profiteers, among other causes, has so reduced the value of currency as to put us at a decided disadvantage in trading with other countries. Class legislation has brought the country to the verge of bankruptcy; and yet when the farmers rise up to cry "Halt!" the press, that has so quietly acquiesced in the wholesale plundering of the country this long while, now wakes up and quite violently voices the fear that the farmers intend only to legislate for their own class. Could anything well be more impudent? It is adding insult to injury with a vengeance, and reminds one of the last damnable straw of which we are told in the proverb.

Class legislation, it must be remembered, has not been confined only to the period of the war.

It was only then (and then only through the complete co-operation of the plutocratic classes) that it reached its climax. But Canada has never at any time known any other kind of legislation than class legislation. It is well known that the plutocrats have dominated political life because they co-operated for their common benefit, or because they were highly organized. Roughly speaking, about five per cent. of our population has, through organization, made the laws which the other ninety-five per cent. had to obey. The exploitation of the natural resources, and the exploitation of labor, have served to produce twenty-three money kings who control the whole arterial system of Canadian commercial life. These kings of commerce and industry are the commanders of the political parties. They dictate the policies, and they make the laws, and they do both in the sole interest of property rights and business. It is because of this class domination by twenty-three money kings that the farmers organized. As was shown in a previous section, when the economic pressure through class legislation became intolerable the farmers banded together to protect their lives. It was, therefore, natural for them to develop a strong antipathy to class rule, and to become the protagonists of industrial and political democracy.

It would be interesting and instructive, if I had the time, to trace in all our laws for the last forty years the influence of class interest. I believe that class interest is behind every one of them. I do not see how it could be otherwise. Our law-makers may have had the purest motives, but they could not help expressing, and consequently protecting, the class to which they belonged. The very fact that it was the good of that class, and no mere personal good, that they had at heart, would prove, indeed, how pure the motives were. I do not blame our law-makers for acting in this way, neither would I advocate that any class should be abolished, nor its just rights interfered with. What is required is that all classes shall be represented, and have an influence on legislation, not one class only.

Examples of class legislation, enacted by and for our twenty-three money kings, are not far to seek. Take the laws, for instance, that deal with the disposition of the natural resources. How did it happen that the money kings got control of the lands, the timber, the minerals, and the fisheries? Or how does it come that there are more laws dealing with the rights of private property than with the health, the education, and the life of the people? Surely because property owners made the laws, and being financially in a position to look after their own health, education, and life, they thought less of others than of themselves, and made their principal business the safe-guarding of their privileges. Or, what better example of class legislation could be found than the tariff? The tariff is of enormous benefit to manufacturers, but of equally enormous disadvantage to everybody else. It was imposed on the nation and kept in force by the manufacturers, in their own interests. Its object was, and is, to increase the profits upon the capital invested in the industry protected. This is, of course, not the reason *given* by the manufacturers, but it *is* the reason. The tariff encourages manufacturers of farm implements, let us say, but at the same time, and in consequence, it discourages all the farmers in Canada who must buy implements at an increased price. How is it, then, that the tariff law which helps to make rich a few while it burdens the many, is still in operation? Because the few that are enriched have the political power. The exercise of this political power results in class legislation. The farmers of Canada have paid to the last farthing the price of this class legislation. The masses have to pay, always, when legislation creates monopoly and makes millionaires of individuals. There is no other way to make millionaires. By the actual suffering of injustice through maladministration the farmer is the most ardent enemy of class rule. Those opposing the United Farmers are unfortunate in their selection of a weapon. The abolition of class rule is the chief aim of the farmers' political endeavor, and as I shall show here, the political methods adopted by them are such as to end government by a favored class.

There are some who will persist in misrepresenting the farmers' movement regardless of whatever information they may have. Whether their information be correct or incorrect, true or false, makes no matter. Against these either protest or denial is useless. They are bent on hindering the movement, and any means that will help them in this object will be fully justified. Falsehood and vilification will be resorted to by them, if thereby their end may be gained. This is the old political game, and, being understood as such, it is not likely to cause much of a setback. It may be suggested, however, in reply to those who are paid to give publicity to the class legislation charge against the farmers, that domination by the agricultural class might, after all, be altogether more desirable than plutocratic domination. Even let it be supposed that the farmers *are* seeking to control the governments in their own interest. What of it? It is their innings, surely. They have been ruled now for a long time. They have been long oppressed. Would it be any the worse for Canada if the farmers should rule for a change, and if, for a change, the oppressors should be oppressed? Even at this low estimate of the farmers' movement, its success could hardly fail to improve conditions for the Canadian people. The agricultural industry is fundamental to the life and prosperity of the nation. If agriculture is successful, as it may be presumed to be under an agrarian class government, all other industries will be—indirectly—benefitted; so that it will be, in any case, much more democratic for Canada to be governed by the agricultural class than by the plutocratic class. At the present time industry and politics in Canada are directed by twenty-three men, or about twenty-three; but with the farmers in control at Ottawa about fifty per cent. of the population would be represented in the ruling class. This would be a great advance for democracy. If Canada is to have class rule, the class to rule indisputably should be the farmers. Their title to the position of ruling class is theirs by right of numbers, by the supreme importance of their industry, and because they have borne far more than their share of the burden of the class rule of the past. What is more, if the farmers desire class rule there is nothing to prevent them from getting it except their own policy.

The group policy, logically followed, will prevent *any* class from dominating. The way to get power as a class is to follow the party method. If the farmers were to deny their class origin and interest, and appeal to all for their support, as the plutocrats do through the old parties, then would the farmers be on the way to imposing on the country a class domination. A farmer will just as surely vote for his own class interest as lawyers and manufacturers have done for theirs. The farmer is just as human, and just as selfish, as other men. If democracy were to depend on the unselfishness of farmers, it would fare little better than it has done under the selfishness of manufacturers. The farmers know this, and frankly admit it. More than that, they make provision against it. They do not say, "Vote for farmers, give *them* the power, and you will be sure to get justice," they say, "Organize your groups, and send your group representatives, along with the farmers' group representatives, to see that you *get* justice." Strange as it may seem, it is this provision made by the farmers against the possibility of class domination that is objected to by the class in power, and its indispensable servant, the press.

Group organization does not imply class legislation. It is the negation of class legislation. It is true that when there is only one group organized they may dominate. That is how the plutocratic class has ruled Canada throughout its history. The business interests were the only group that was organized to that point of efficiency that commanded power. But such a condition is passing away. It is the challenge to the present ruling class given by the organized farmers that is the basis of all the objection. The more organized groups there are, the less chance for any one group to control affairs in its own interest. The Manufacturers' Association sees this and protests against the farmers' group organization; the farmers see it too, and advise all groups to organize, and to organize without delay.

Group organization is the natural outcome of democratic development. The common economic interest supplied by the industrial pursuit is the binding factor which holds people together. The fact that different people, of different ages, and with different thoughts, are held bound by their common industrial interest, strengthens the organization. The varied opinions harmonized in the general interest make creative social thinking possible without disrupting the group or democratic unit. Group organization is suffering in some quarters to-day because of its honesty. It admits the selfishness implied in class interest; it would be hypocritical, false, and foolish to deny it. Some people seem to think they can get rid of selfishness by denying its existence. As a matter of fact, there is less selfishness in an organized group than in the mass of unorganized individuals, for the individual who has become part of a group has sunk his immediate self-interest to the extent, at least, that he thinks in and acts for a group, whereas before, he thought and acted for himself alone. The farmers are selfish and admit it. They are not any more nor any less selfish than other people. This is acknowledged, but it is claimed, also, that it is simply because of class selfishness that all classes must be represented in parliament before justice is possible. The farmers, recognizing this, are preparing to play their part. Their group organization principle, when extended to other classes, will make class legislation impossible.

That group representation will lead to cooperation instead of class rule is obvious. Suppose that there are three classes represented in parliament, the farmers, the industrial workers, and the commercial interests. There will be other classes ultimately, but these three classes already are factors to be reckoned with. Well, we will suppose each class to be selfish and to want more than its share. When one of them attempts out of all reason to legislate for itself, what will happen? What can happen but that the selfishness of the other two classes will combine to prevent the legislation of the first class from becoming operative. The only check on the selfishness of the one class is the selfishness of the other two. Thus the competition which has hitherto taken place between individuals will take place between groups, and will lead to a higher order of co-operation. As we have seen in our "Chain of Social Progress" section, competition plays an important part in development. It is practised among individuals, and groups, and nations, until it becomes destructive and threatens the life of all. It then yields place to co-operation, which comes naturally and of necessity. Fortunately, it will not be necessary for the representatives of the various groups in a parliament to go through a long experience of class conflict before they realize the virtue of co-operation. Of course, if they do not know the laws of human relations, experience will be necessary. But the experience already common on the lower planes of co-operation will be sufficient to warrant the adoption of a higher co-operation among the groups. The farmers know now that co-operation is the goal towards which they are striving. They are working consciously toward it. They are following the natural path, and if they do not leave it, their destiny is certain. Group organization is the natural course. Group representation is the only way to avoid class legislation. The coming together of the representatives of the various groups is the only way by which co-operation can be extended to government.

To sum up the main points of this section: Canada has always suffered from class legislation; it is therefore a *reductio ad absurdum* for that class which has ruled, in its own behalf, throughout the history of the country, to charge the farmers, before they have secured a dozen representatives in parliament, with the deliberate intention of ruling in their own behalf, when it was the economic pressure of class legislation, on the part of the present ruling class, which led the farmers to organize in the first place. One of the chief political aims of the farmers is to abolish class rule; but if class rule is our highest social achievement, and one that cannot be abolished, the farmers, by mere right of numbers, should be the class to rule in Canada. Their importance to the state, and the fact that they constitute over half the population is warrant enough. But class rule *can* be abolished. Group organizations, advocating the self-determination of industrial groups, and insisting on the right of minorities to representation, will, in the end, overwhelm both the theory and the fact of class domination, and lead to the establishment in governmental affairs, of co-operation between the groups.

§6

Farmers' Platform not Class Law. I have tried to show, theoretically, that there are no reasonable grounds to fear class legislation from the United Farmers. My conclusions rest upon the hypothesis of the group philosophy. I turn, now, to consider the charge of class legislation from the only practical standpoint possible to one holding my views—that is, the standpoint provided by the farmers' platform. What has it to say to the Canadian people on class legislation? Being really a *farmers'* platform, representing the social thought of the organized farmers of Canada, its testimony should be of great value in our investigation of the charges made by partisans.

The farmers' platform has been called by some "The New National Policy." This name was a concession to the prejudice created by the enemies of the farmers' movement, but it emphasizes the democratic nature of the legislature proposed by the movement. The farmers' platform cannot be a national policy in the sense of being all-inclusive. There are other groups, whose platforms, while not opposing the principles set forth by the farmers, include principles which the farmers have overlooked. Liberals, Conservatives, Unionists, Farmers, the labor organizations, and the Socialists, all have platforms. It would require the best of these, and perhaps of many others besides to make a national policy that would really be national in the sense of expressing the needs of the whole people. The farmers' platform, therefore, can be considered a national policy only in the sense that in all that it proposes it aims at the service of the nation. It is composed of national needs as seen by the farmers. That there are other national needs, which will be more readily seen by other groups, is but natural. An examination of the farmers' platform will justify its claim to be a new national policy, in that it will be seen to aim at national service, and will also give the *quietus* to those who seek to besmirch the farmers' political movement by imputing to it "narrow," "selfish," "sordid," and "class," designs.

The first demand of the farmers, in their platform, is for a League of Nations "to give permanence to the world's peace by removing old causes of conflict." It is not necessary to defend this against the charge of being a "class" demand. The peace of the world is of equal interest to the people of all nations. The wide outlook and the foresight implied in this ideal are democratic and indicative of the fitness of the farmers to have a share in directing national and international matters. This plank may be safely committed to the rough seas of criticism without further observation. Its merit as a solution of international problems is already the subject of volumes. I am concerned with it here merely as evidence against the charges of class intrigue brought against the farmers by those opposed to their political aspirations.

The next declaration in the platform is sequential. It deals with imperialism. If "old causes of conflict" are to be removed, imperialism will have to go. The farmers know this and have declared against it. They say: "We believe that the further development of the British Empire should be sought along the lines of partnership between nations free and equal. . . . We are strongly opposed to any attempt to centralize imperial control. Any attempt to set up an independent authority with power to bind the Dominions, whether this authority be termed parliament, council, or cabinet, would hamper the growth of responsible and informed democracy in the Dominions." Here is a definite renunciation of imperialism, coupled with the demand that Canada, as a free nation, be given equal status with Great Britain in any partnership which may be arranged for the benefit of both. Is this a narrow class desire? Does it not give utterance to a national sentiment which cannot much longer be repressed? Doubtless, if the "knavish tricks" of imperialists are frustrated, a few people will be deprived of fond and remunerative ambitions. But certain it is that in national freedom there is no exclusive benefit for the farmers. There is no circumscribed class selfishness in a desire for national equality. It implies the welfare of Canada, and in any other country would be called patriotic.

Next in order, on the farmers' program, come the tariff declarations. The protective tariff is denounced as "fostering combines in almost every line of Canadian industrial enterprise." The farmers claim that by it the people are exploited, and that agriculture, the basic industry, is so handicapped as to be an unprofitable pursuit, in consequence of which rural populations are being depleted. As a revenue producer the tariff is costly. Its chief virtue is that it puts three dollars into the pockets of the protected interests for every one that it puts into the public treasury. As a privilege the tariff is immoral and accounts for much of the corruption of our public life. Those who would, in their own interests, maintain the tariff, are willing to spend for political purposes money by means of which both parties in the past have been corrupted, and are corrupted still. Apart from the class interests that are protected by it, the tariff has no justification. In declaring against the tariff, the farmers are repudiating class legislation, and doing a service to all. If the farmer is more affected by a tax upon commodities than the average individual, that is because in his line of work he must buy more. But directly and indirectly, every individual living in Canada must suffer from tariffs, and legislation reducing or abolishing them must, of necessity, be of immense benefit to all. In no sense can the tariff policy of the Canadian Council of Agriculture be interpreted as a special privilege to farmers. Is it class legislation to set free from taxation the food and clothing of working people, when that tax enriches individuals at the expense of the masses who have neither enough to eat nor wear? Is it class legislation to remove from between nations trade restrictions that not only interfere with natural prosperity but are the prolific source of wars as long as they are retained? Is it class legislation to remove from farm machinery the toll that has no other effect than to reduce production, to impoverish the farmers, and to raise the cost of living all round? No! It is class legislation to maintain this injustice, and that is why the farmers want to abolish it.

Direct taxation for revenue is the farmers' substitute method. They advocate "a tax on unimproved land values, including all natural resources." As the result of such a tax would be to force the people now holding natural resources out of use to develop such natural resources, its introduction would inevitably be of general advantage. It does strike at class privilege, not in the interests of the farmers' class alone, but in the interest of every class except the one that now rules the roost. It is estimated that the total land values of Canada amount to $8,000,000,000. A tax of one per cent. on Canadian land values would produce a revenue of $80,000,000. By removing taxation from commodities and placing it on land, the cost of living would be reduced at once, while eventually the tax on land would result in greatly increased production and ever greater national prosperity. Further provision is made for revenue by a "graduated income tax." As this tax falls upon every individual who has an income, it includes all farmers; and as the tax is graduated it will fall justly upon each according to his ability to pay. It will be a further check on privilege.

It is also proposed to place "a graduated inheritance tax on large estates." This proposal strikes at hereditary wealth on the principle that enormous wealth cannot justly be gained by an individual; that, when an individual laying claim to the ownership of wealth dies, the state has a claim upon such wealth; and that those unfortunate enough to inherit wealth should be saved from its demoralizing influence, and be obliged to work for a living. The "graduated income tax on the profits of corporations," another suggestion brought forward by the United Farmers, will increase the national revenue still further; it will, also, discourage large profits, and by so doing will confer a favor on the population as a whole.

The principle of direct taxation is just and democratic. The specific proposals so far made on the basis of this principle are advantageous to the masses. In these matters the farmers seek no special privilege, they challenge the right of privileges to exist at all, and deeming their existence wrong, take steps towards curtailing them.

The platform deals at length, and in detail, with the returned soldier. Methods of demobilization, and of the re-establishment in their pre-war vocations of the returned men who are physically fit, are advocated. Vocational training, insurance at the public expense for men without pensions who have become undesirable insurance risks, the provision of facilities necessary to enable soldiers to settle on the land, and other desirable legislation in the interest of returned soldiers, are also demanded. I place this on the side of the scales weighing against class legislation without further comment. Let those who claim to have contrary arguments, throw them into the opposite balance.

The remaining portions of the farmers' platform are so obviously *anti-class,* and so positively democratic, that I need but quote them. "A land settlement scheme based on a regulating influence on the selling price of land. Owners of idle areas should be obliged to file a selling price on their lands, that price also to be regarded as an assessable value for purposes of taxation; extension of co-operative agencies in agriculture to cover the whole field of marketing, including arrangements with consumers' societies for the supplying of foodstuffs at the lowest rates and with the minimum of middleman handling; public ownership and control of railway, water and aerial transportation, telephone, telegraph, and express systems, all projects in the development of natural power, and of the coal mining industry."

In dealing with political democracy, the following reforms are advocated: "The discontinuance of the practice of conferring titles upon citizens of Canada; the reform of the federal Senate; an immediate check upon the growth of government by order-in-council, and increased responsibility of individual members of parliament in all legislation, the complete abolition of the patronage system, the publication of contributions and expenditures both before and after election campaigns, the setting forth by daily newspapers and periodical publications of the facts of their ownership and control; proportional representation; the establishment of measures of direct legislation through the initiative, referendum and recall; the opening of parliament to women on the same terms as men."

Much might be said on the democratic merits of each clause above quoted, but to point these out would be to go beyond the purpose of this enquiry, which is to consider the farmers' platform from the viewpoint of class legislation. In this respect it speaks for itself, clearly and decisively. Where is the person who will undertake to substantiate from this platform the charge of class legislation? He, or she, does not exist. This challenge cannot be accepted.

There is not one clause in the political principles of the farmers' platform but refutes the class charges of the movement's opponents.

The nature of the farmers' organization strikes at class domination; the spirit of the farmers' program is just and democratic; the farmers have never had an opportunity to govern, so cannot be faced with deeds of class advantage. Where, then, is the excuse for the accusation of class legislation? No honest excuse exists. The reason the accusation is made is that by false charges against its antagonists votes may be gained for the present ruling class. The farmers who have made their own platform with democratic intent, and who desire fair representation for all classes will not be turned aside from their path by the worn-out, disreputable tactics of party politics, but will move onward, unperturbed by temporary difficulties and setbacks, assured that in the end victory is certain.

§7

The Alternative. There is only one constitutional alternative to group representation in parliament, and that is to continue the party system. Groups are superseding parties by a natural development corresponding to the growing complexity of civilization. But the party habit of thought is strong, even though sentiment is against it. It is possible to meet with ardent haters of the party system who unconsciously adopt the party methods in combating partyism.

The United Farmers originated as an industrial group. Apart from the group idea, the farmers' movement has no meaning and no future. Its spirit is anti-party and co-operative. But this notwithstanding, party methods and tactics are still advocated by many in the farmers' group. If the party methods are adopted, the farmers as a group will cease to exist. Politically, the farmers must either be content to send their own representatives to parliament, to co-operate in government with the representatives of other groups, or they must become a party, claiming the ability to represent all groups, and strive to become a government. There is no alternative.

Those who would convert the farmers' movement into a National Party are sincere. They, also, are opposed to the party system, but are afraid of the group in politics because it lacks the qualities leading to immediate popularity. These "New Party" supporters want to abolish partyism, but would build a new and stronger party with which to do it. They are in the same position as the destroyers of militarism who build one military system to defeat another, only to find, after defeating it, that they are left with a greater militarism of their own. The adherents of this outworn creed are still within the vicious circle of party politics, and when they are most hopeful of getting out they are the most hopelessly shut in. That circle is like the spider's web. Pity the poor fly that gets into it!

The most undemocratic phase of partyism is its aim at complete power. The full control of the state is the ambition of all parties, and it is because of this control that the plutocratic class is careful by some means or other to command the party strong enough to form the government. Democratically speaking, no party has the right to govern. In a democracy there can only be a partnership in power. The right of a party to form a government is the right of might, might of propaganda, of manipulation, or of numbers. The party that has one vote more than another assumes the right to rule, as though justice resided in a majority. The industrial group in politics does not seek to become all-powerful in the state. It seeks representation, or a share in administration. If there is going to be a government, it must either be controlled autocratically, by the strongest party, or conducted co-operatively by the representatives of the people. All political movements to-day support either autocratic party domination, or group co-operative government, and it would be well if those who desire co-operation in government, while they adopt the party method, would explain how they expect to attain their end. The onus is upon those who repudiate the group to show the difference between a farmers' party and any other party.

The United Farmers in contemplation of political action have before them either course. If the path which leads to party government be taken, little of value will be attained, and the whole democratic fight will have to be fought over again. It may take thousands of years to accomplish co-operation. Time is no object to nature. But no matter if it takes a million years, it cannot take place until the proper elements of co-operation have been developed. They are now appearing in the form of industrial groups. Their appearance implies the disintegration of the party system, and the formation of a new alignment on a co-operative basis. The farmers' organization is one of the new units. If it is recognized and maintained, other units of a similar nature will arise, and co-operation will result. But if the group be disowned and disregarded in favor of a party and power, democracy must wait. The group will have to be rebuilt. As to whether the group is disowned or not, that depends upon the ripeness of the time and the readiness of the people concerned. If they are not ready, civilization will have to wait until they are.

I will not deny that a new farmer's party organized on the old party plan may accomplish minor reforms. Every new party or new government does that, and if the farmers' party were in power in Canada, we might expect a period of honest effort, at least. Such a government would be conservative, and therefore would hardly sponsor much rash legislation; it would be as unsophisticated as a country girl entering so-called society; its natural honesty would be wholesome and beneficial; it is reasonable, too, to suppose that a farmers' government would materially reduce, or perhaps even abolish the tariff, and pass other legislation that would be in the interests of agriculture. As a party, however, it would ultimately assume the features of preceding parties. The first shot of the nettle is tender, soft, and harmless, but it *is* a *nettle,* and give it but time to grow and it cannot help but sting. The fact that a party is a *farmers'* party will not prevent it from bearing fruit according to its kind. Power has a wonderful fascination. Once enjoyed by a farmers' party it would be sought after to the exclusion of all else. In order to hold on to it, the party would have to cater to certain influences, and by and by would be as corrupt as its rivals. With a farmers' party in power, the Liberals and Conservatives would join and we would be back to the old two-party system with its lust for authority, with its servility to class interests, with its corruption and autocracy. If a movement is steered in the party course, it cannot hope for a different destiny.

It is what the farmers' movement is in itself, that is going to count. If it can be made into something else it will lose its significance and fail to make its contribution. As a product of natural conditions, the farmers' movement cannot be destroyed, not even by those of its members who may not grasp its full meaning. It cannot really be made into anything else. At the worst the good of which it is capable can only be delayed. Its first great lesson is that society is composed of industrial groups which must act as units in co-operation for mutual well-being. The party view is that society is divided into two classes. The Socialists also held the two class view—though with a difference. The Socialists' idea is that the two classes must fight until one secures the mastery over the other, after which there will be only one class, or more correctly speaking, no class—the future belongs to the people. The political party view is that there are two classes, that they fight each other, that they exist to fight each other always, and that political parties must, also, exist as their armies to do the fighting. The difference between the Socialists and the orthodox political parties is that the Socialist holds that some day the working class will completely do away with the capitalist class, while the political parties think the struggle is endless, but with plutocracy always on the top. The class struggle of doctrinaire Socialism is acknowledged and accepted by both capitalist and Socialist. Class war will go on until the self-determination of the last class in society is assured.

It is false to hold to a two-class theory of society on an economic basis. I maintain this, even though Karl Marx denies it. The two classes are supposed to be the haves and the have-nots, the workers and the capitalists, the slaves and the masters. But society may be divided by other methods, economically as sound, into two very different classes. For instance, society might be divided into the foolish and the wise, the sick and the healthy, or the living and the dead. The wise, the healthy, and the living, would be in each case the privileged class, and should, according to the class struggle, fight its opposite. But health, wisdom, and life, are not to be gained by over-throwing those possessing them. Neither can justice be established by one class overthrowing another, any more than defeat of the Tories by the Liberals brings democracy.

The fact is that there are a great many economic classes in society. Let us suppose that capital and labor have had their final struggle, and labor has been victorious. What then? There will still be farmers, miners, transportation workers, and a great number of other skilled and unskilled classes in competition with each other over the spoils of capitalism. The farmer would want as much as possible in exchange for his wheat, the miner would want the most he could get in exchange for the coal he mined, and the transport worker who hauled the coal and the wheat would also want for his work all he could obtain. Now, if the farmers could exchange half a sack of wheat instead of a whole sack for two sacks of coal, there would be less wheat for the miner and the railroad worker. The fight, therefore, after the overthrow of capital exploitation, would go merrily on even as before.

Capitalism to-day may be the common enemy of all industrial groups. These groups may and will co-operate in the overthrow of the individualistic system, just as Great Britain, France, the United States, Canada, and other countries co-operated to defeat Germany in the Great War. But there is nothing constructive in the defeating of Germany nor in the overthrowing of capitalism. The downfall of capitalism is just as certain to take place as the downfall of Germany was. Capitalism will fall, but not by the efforts of the dispossessed. It will be slain by its own hand. But what concerns us most is the New System that is to replace capitalism. That new system must recognize the many existing classes, and provide self-determination for each. A government on the basis of no class would be as false as a government on the basis of two classes. All classes must be recognized. The real classes are the industrial groups, and of these there are as many as there are industries.

The two-party system of government presupposes the two-class interpretation of society. The development of groups seeking political recognition is the best proof of the two-class fallacy. The greatest contribution that the farmers could possibly make would be the maintenance of their group identity together with the co-operative philosophy which necessarily follows from it. Shall the possibility of a co-operative state be bartered for the momentary pleasure of political power? This is the question which must be answered by the farmers' movement, in the near future. Shall representation be sought with a view to co-operation, or a party be built up for the sake of power? There is no other course. The perpetuation of partyism is the only alternative to the co-operative group system.

§8

Group Government. The party system is now on trial. The evidence against it is strong and convincing, and shows it to be a government device that was suitable to a bygone age. New conditions and complications, however, have arisen which throw it out of touch with the people's real needs. Further evidence shows the party system to have been an outgrowth of autocracy; shows also, that it does not represent the people; that it is controlled by the wealthy; and that it is corrupt. With such a weight of evidence against it the verdict is almost certain to be one of "Guilty."

Throughout the Dominion of Canada the antipathy to partyism is very pronounced. So pronounced, indeed, that the old parties are changing their names, and new parties, in a last effort to preserve the system, are hastily being put forward. Everywhere in the political world signs may be seen portending changes in the form of government that will bring government into line with the great changes that are taking place in industry, education, religion, and political organization. As I have tried to show, the party system, with the development of new conditions, is becoming obsolete. The greatest indictment of it is that it does not work; it cannot be made to serve the developed democratic ideals. The criticism of one part by another, although attracting public attention to party corruption, would not be sufficient to discredit so entirely the party system. It is the inherent inability of the system to serve the best interests of a modern nation that condemns it.

If the party system is going, what is to take its place when it is gone? Reasonable people will ask this question. The answer to it is not obscure. In fact, the party system is being pushed to the wall and crowded out by the new form of organization which is even now pressing for "a place in the sun." What took the place of partyism in the constituencies of North Dakota, in the United States, and in Ontario, and various federal ridings throughout the Canadian West? The farmers' group organization. The place of party organization among the people is being filled by group organization. In varying degrees this is true not of Canada only, but of the civilized world. What we have to ask ourselves now is if it is reasonable to suppose that, since party organization led to party government, group organization will lead to group government? Party organization developed at a time when it was needed. Group organization is as natural a product of our time as party organization was of the days of old. As the necessity changes, so changes the organization. Group organization is a fact, it is not a theory. The industrial groups in Canada, organized farmers and organized labor, are seeking representation in parliament. If these groups obtain representation in parliament, whether we want it or not, we shall have a group parliament. There is no need to preach group government. Given the group organization in the constituencies the form of government will look after itself.

It is not my intention to outline in detail a group government. The hint given by Robert Burns in his verse concerning "the plans of mice and men" is sufficient to cool the ardor of any government manufacturer. The new form of government cannot be constructed beforehand by any individual. Suffice it to say that the group government which will result from the new forms of political organization must be molded to fit the new conditions. It will be a natural outgrowth of group representation, and will have to accommodate itself to its group environment. Governments in the air are castles in Spain. I shall not, therefore, occupy space with worthless detail while there are general principles involved, that may be considered with more profit. Every political tendency is toward some form of group government. The inefficiency of the party system, the widespread and determined opposition to it; the growing tendency on the part of industrial groups to ignore party governments, and to look to their own organizations for redress; and the coming into parliament of representatives of industrial groups, all justify the conclusion that Canada will not only have a new personnel in the legislature in the near future, but that the government itself will be new. That government will be a group government, because it will be composed of representatives of organized groups.

A party government will no longer be possible

when several groups by co-operation are found to be stronger than the party in power. No amount of advocacy will bring about a group government, nor will volumes of criticism prevent it if the conditions are present. The organization of groups is a fact. Bankers, manufacturers, and other business interests are organized on a class basis; labor constitutes an industrial group—the farmers another group. Proportional Representation will tend to give these and other groups representation according to numerical strength. It does not require much imagination to realize that with organized groups and the proportional representation system of voting the whole structure of parliament will be changed. In the legislative assembly there will be as many groups as there are definite economic interests. How could the two-party system function under such conditions?

It is reasonable to think that if proportional representation is applied to the groups outside of parliament it will have to be applied to the groups within parliament as well. Otherwise, what would be the advantage of proportional voting? The logical outcome of proportional voting will be proportional responsibility in government. It will have to be applied in the assembly as well as in the constituency. If it is democratic to have represented in parliament every group that is numerically strong enough to poll the quota of votes under proportional representation in the constituencies, it must also be democratic to have every group in parliament proportionately represented in the Cabinet.

A group government, as I conceive it, implies that each group would be represented in the Cabinet. No group of any strength would be able to shirk responsibility, as, under the two-party system, is done by the opposition. The group government might be represented as a circle. The Cabinet or Executive, which will be as representative of the assembly as the assembly is of the people as a whole, will be the center of the circle. Just as the center of a circle is equidistant from any point in its circumference, so would responsibility be placed equally upon every group within the circle of parliament. Thus the British principle of responsible government would not be impaired, but safeguarded and extended. While a party government is held responsible for its action, it must not be forgotten that, in many cases, nearly half the assembly has no responsibility whatsoever. Having no responsibility, the tactics of the opposition is usually such as to embarrass those who do have responsibility.

Why should there be an opposition artificially fixed? A perpetual opposition, such as the two-party system produces, is ridiculous. It implies that everything attempted by the government is wrong, and that an opposition has prevision of every measure introduced by the government throughout its term of office. Everybody knows that neither of these implications is correct. Governments do not always do wrong, neither does the opposition know beforehand what it is going to be called upon to oppose. Therefore, party opposition is immoral, for it means that a member may have to oppose measures his own conscience favors; and it is, also, unintelligent because it has no regard for the merits of any question under discussion. For these reasons parliamentary debates have long been looked upon as farcical.

I do not claim that there will be no opposition in a group government. But I maintain that there will be no opposition for opposition's sake. It will be honest and intelligent. It will depend upon the issue, and the personnel of the opposition may change as that changes. Parliamentary debate will have meaning, because every issue will be in doubt until the vote is taken, and not decided in caucus before being presented for the consideration of the assembly. It will be decided on its merits instead of by a counting of party heads, as is done in our parliaments to-day.

The situation in the Ontario legislature, after the election of 1919, is interesting from the group government point of view. In the house there are four groups. No group is strong enough to form a party government, and it is only by forming a Coalition that a majority of one can be secured. The farmers' group, being the largest of the four, followed the party custom, and undertook to form a government with the aid of the labor group. No attempt was made to deal with the situation in the manner here suggested, and the presence of four groups in the legislature notwithstanding, the Ontario government was formed on a party basis. In consequence, its existence is precarious. If it lasts a four year term it will be because the opposing groups have nothing to gain by upsetting it.

DEMOCRACY AND THE GROUP

There are two questions to be asked, relating to Premier Drury's administration. The first is, Why should Premier Drury and his group have felt called upon to assume the whole responsibility for the government of Ontario, just because the farmers' group was stronger by a few members than any of the other groups? It must be kept in mind that the Drury group represents but a minority of the voting population of the province, and that the representatives of the majority of the electorate have no share in the administration. The second question is, Why should the Liberal and Conservative groups in the Ontario legislature, when they represent a majority of the people, have been excluded from their share of governmental responsibility? There are no satisfactory answers to these questions. All four groups were elected for the same purpose, namely, to take part in the government of Ontario. There is no good reason why two of them should be exempted from sharing that responsibility; neither can the acceptance of power by a coalition representing a minority of the people be justified either on democratic or any other grounds. These things are excused by the party system of government, but justified they cannot be. Premier Drury formed a government on the two-party system, ignoring the new factors which have entered the legislature, and which render party government more difficult and more undemocratic than it was before.

All the conditions for the formation of a group government were present in Ontario. Each group should have been called upon to provide representation for the Cabinet in proportion to its strength in the legislature, and to accept its share of governmental responsibility. But the people were not ready. They will not be ready until the groups in parliament demonstrate that the two-party system cannot function in a four-party legislature. I have no intention of casting a reflection upon Premier Drury. His task was great and difficult. I believe that he was in favor of a group government, while the others were not ready. Would the Conservatives and Liberals have agreed to a group government proposal? It is doubtful if they would. They do not look upon the presence of the agrarian and labor groups as permanent factors. The old parties think that the advent of these groups is incidental to an after-the-war psychology, and that the parties will be restored in the near future. The tactics of the two-party opposition in Ontario are, therefore, to permit the industrial coalition government to go on until the tide of public opinion swings, as they expect, back to the dear old parties. But that swing back will never take place. The two new groups in the Ontario legislature are organized upon an industrial basis and are permanent. Their numbers may vary in succeeding elections, but they will have representation. As time goes on, the industrial organizations will be solidified, extended, and perfected, thus insuring representation for the agriculturalists and the industrial workers. It is probable that when it becomes known that farmers and laborers have come to parliament to stay Conservatives and Liberals will be more favorable to the formation of a government in keeping with the new conditions.

But the old parties in Ontario were not the only barriers in the way of a group government. It may be said, with truth, that neither the United Farmers nor the Labor organization were conscious of the full significance of what was taking place. They did not associate the new and additional political factors created by themselves, with a change in the governmental system. Neither of the groups which combined to form the Drury administration expected to be called upon to act as administrators. For the victory of the farmers, the unjust system of voting was responsible, and as the farmers had no expectation of capturing the government, methods and forms of government were never discussed in the locals, so that not even the farmers themselves were prepared for a group government. It is for this reason that I now adumbrate the group government idea. The *details* of such a government must be worked out *by* such a government, but it may be shown to be the logical outcome of the advent of industrial groups in politics. It must be brought before the people for consideration and study, so that they will be ready to make the change most efficiently when the time arrives.

Group government is not practicable and cannot be formed when there are only two parties. But, when four or five groups take the place of two parties in the legislature, what is going to be done? Either a group government, which will be fair to all, must be formed, or else we will continue to till our modern political fields with antediluvian implements. But I believe that conditions very shortly will make the introduction of group government a necessity. Let us imagine what would have happened had the Liberals of Ontario secured the strongest representation in the election of 1919. With whom would they have coalesced? It may be doubted whether the Conservative, the farmer, or the labor representatives would have condescended to form a coalition with the Liberals. Or if the Conservatives had secured the largest group, there would have been the same dilemma. "Back to the people" would have been the cry. A new election, however, would have made little difference, because the new industrial groups, which were the cause of the political complications, were organized for a definite purpose, and would have stood substantially the same. What then? Would those four groups have sat and looked at each other without making any attempt to govern the province, or would they have discovered the solution in co-operation and formed a group government? The dilemma is possible still, and a way out of it may have to be found in Ontario after the next provincial election. What will be the outcome? If the people study the situation as it is, and are acquainted with the idea of group government as the logical procedure, group government will come just as naturally as the two-party government came, and will have the same relation to our political conditions as party government, at its inception, had to the political conditions then existing.

A group government of some sort, it cannot be said too often, will be the necessary outcome of political action on the part of industrial groups. If industrial group organizations continue, as there is every reason to believe they will, and if they seek and obtain representation in parliament as they are doing, the two-party system will have to go. When the party system goes, either group government or a military dictatorship will have to supersede it. In view of the nature of the alternative it is most likely that group government will be welcomed by all.

Group government when established will imply a partnership in power, in administration, and responsibility. I do not pretend to foresee the methods that will be adopted in selecting cabinets, nor to outline a system of parliamentary procedure for a group government. These will take care of themselves. The essential difference between a group and a party government in action will be that, instead of one faction undertaking to govern all, as is the practice to-day, every faction, party, or group in the legislative assembly will share in governing; instead of all power being in the hands of one party, representing, as only too often is the case, but a minority of the people, the power will be held jointly by all representatives of the people; and instead of competition in government we shall have co-operation. Such a government would be compatible with the nature of modern political organization, and also with the proportional representation system of electing representatives.

To attempt further details would be presumptuous. There are, however, certain democratic principles necessary to a group government, which might be emphasized. Representative government has been the boasted glory of the British system. That principle is soundly democratic. It is a principle upon the closest possible adherence to which depends national harmony. The political organizations, and the election methods of the past, have defeated the traditional ideal of representative government.

It is because the party organization and its corollary, party government, make true representative government impossible, that we have new political uprisings. Canadian governments do not represent the people. If all the people in Canada were lawyers and manufacturers and business men, our governments would be representative, and there would be no political unrest. But these professional and plutocratic classes represent a very small section of the population. The Canadian government, at any time, represents at the most not more than ten per cent. of the Canadian people. The ninety per cent. has no representation. The fallacy that a person from one class can represent all other classes is the basis of the party system. There is no need to demonstrate this fallacy. Forty years of legislation by one class in Canada is an irrefutable argument against its continuance. Ordinary commonsense is sufficient to show how impossible it is for a lawyer, a manufacturer, or a banker to represent and legislate for all industrial groups. A manufacturer does not consider the farmer when he passes a tariff law, because, in the first place, he is representing the manufacturers, and in the second place, he knows nothing of agricultural needs, and is too much out of touch to act justly, no matter how much he may wish to do so. Farmers can only be represented by farmers, labor can only be represented by labor, and business can only be represented by business men. In a representative government all are needed.

Group organization, and its necessary corollary, group government, will bring to fruition this long admired British principle which is thoroughly democratic and scrupulously just. Everyone who knows and appreciates British sentiment desires the fullest measure of representative government. Is there any other way to obtain it but by group organization, group representation, and government by co-operative groups? If there is, I wait for those who are wedded to the party system to reveal it.

The old traditional parliamentary practice that demands the resignation of a government on the defeat of a government measure is necessary to the party system. It was inaugurated as a means of making someone, or some party, responsible for legislation. I cannot conceive of a party government without this. That this practice has recently been ignored in the British

House of Commons is but another evidence that partyism is drifting out. While the practice was intended to hold a government responsible for its actions, it has been used as a means of monopoly and permitted the government to do as it pleased without being responsible to anybody but the plutocratic classes in control of the party governing. The possibility of defeating the government on a legislative measure has become the real party whip. This whip is laid across the back of every government supporter. Those voting contrary to the government must risk their own seats in parliament, as well as accept the responsibility or blame for flinging the country into an unnecessary election. For these reasons a government is seldom defeated by a vote in the house.

Owing to this the members have no freedom. The issue itself is secondary, the life of the government tied up with the issue becomes the important thing. It is hardly conceivable that so stupid a practice should be in vogue in this age of democratic enlightenment, but it is. Under group government the issue would be separated both from individuals and governments. It would be defeated or sustained on its merits.

The government would live out its allotted span of life unless it were necessary to kill it on a vote of no confidence.

A group government composed of representatives of industrial groups would tackle the economic problems that account for the injustice, the poverty, and the consequent unrest of our times. The better day of our dreams, the living together in harmony, are impossible unless the economic system is changed so as to permit these happier conditions. Once more, let me insist that the economic problems are fundamental. There can be no solution of our difficulties until the economic questions are settled on a co-operative basis, and the industrial exploitation of one class by another is done with. Politicians cannot change the economic system. Politicians, to-day, represent those who benefit by the system. There are only two courses open to civilization. We may go on as we are and reap bloody revolution, or we may, by sane, constitutional means, adopt a system of economic justice and economic freedom. One class cannot solve the economic problems of Canada. They will take the co-operation of all classes to solve. Co-operation is the solution for the economic servitude of the masses. When the representatives of the various industrial groups meet around one common government table, each with his, or her, responsibility, both to the group and to the nation as a whole, co-operation will open the door to a new era of Canadian liberty. Then, and only then, will class legislation be abolished; then, and only then, will economic problems be admitted, faced, and settled on a basis making for the well-being of all. Which will Canada choose? Class domination through party government with red revolution at the end, or class organization, class representation and class co-operation for national harmony? As I see it, there is no other alternative. The present unrest is a portent of the future. A representative government will save the day. It must represent all classes, or fail to recognize the grievances of those excluded. Numerous interests are not incompatible with harmony, but are indeed the prerequisites of harmony. Modern conditions advise us that diverse interests must walk together that their diversities may be changed into reciprocities and good understanding take the place of enmity.

My present effort must not be taken as a complete treatise on a new form of government. I intend in another book to deal with that subject more thoroughly. Emphasis, for the time being, must be placed upon the obtaining of group representation. A group government will become necessary only when representatives of groups appear in the various legislative bodies. My main contention with regard to group government is simply this: that if the two old parties centuries ago found a suitable system of government, a system which corresponded both to the prevailing economic conditions and to the form of political organization that existed, it is reasonable to suppose that the different political organizations of modern times, which are springing up in response to changes in our economic life, will not only lead to a corresponding change in the form of government, but also that our modern representatives will be as competent to make the necessary governmental adjustments as were the parliamentarians of other days.

THE CARLETON LIBRARY